Happiness

HOW, WHEN & WHY

Understanding and Maintaining the Essence of Being

Vaibhav Gupta

BlueRose
Publishers
NewDelhi • London

First Published in December 2021

ISBN: 978-93-5472-668-2

BLUEROSE PUBLISHERS
www.bluerosepublishers.com
info@bluerosepublishers.com
+91 8882 898 898

Cover Design:
Shreya

Typographic Design:
Namrata Saini

Distributed by: BlueRose, Amazon, Flipkart, Shopclues

"To my beloved Grandmother Late Meena Devi and Grandfather Late Ganpat Rai – your love remains the foundation to everything I try to do!"

Contents

Acknowledgement

- I offer my sincerest gratitude to my spiritual master and guru <u>His Holiness Sri Sri Ravi Shankar</u> whose teachings and wisdom have served as the foundation to how and what I am today. His teachings have inspired me to live the life of integrity I now live.

- My parents, Archana and Rakesh Gupta, have been a constant source of support. It is with infinite gratitude that I dedicate this work to my beloved parents, without whom I wouldn't be here, or in fact, anywhere at all.

- My brother and sister-in-law, Gaurav and Nidhi, have always supported me unconditionally, and I thank them with all my heart. My nephew and niece, Naman and Yashvi, have filled me with more joy than I could have imagined.

- My rock, my inspiration, my world, my wife Kavita was always there and has supported me always. To have been married to a woman of such a dynamic nature has inspired me to strive every day to live up to that. My son Divyam has brought nothing but joy into my life. I am proud of him for being the kind of son he is.

- I want to thank my parents-in-law, Santosh and Satish Jindal, for welcoming me into the fold. For the last sixteen years, I have always felt that I truly belonged to this family. For all this love, respect and acceptance, I want to express my endless gratitude.

- I want to offer special thanks to Megha, Saras, Ashish, Samaika, Rimaya, my uncle and aunt, Rajesh and Manjari, who have been there for me when I needed them the most and kind to me always. I am thankful for what they have done motivating me.

- I want to thank my friends Vipul, Priyanka, Manish, Poonam, Sushil, Nidhi, Tarun and Payal, who have been a huge part of my life and I am so grateful for everything they have done to encourage me.

- Thanks to Dr Bindu Kohli, a teacher, mentor, sister, and a friend to me who has shown me the way to self-transformation. She has been like a candle to me that brings light by burning itself.

- Binay Kumar, a Permaculture and Yoga teacher, who taught me the ancient yogic practices and kriyas. He encouraged me to serve and engage in sustainable living. I offer my limitless thanks to him.

- I want to thank Pinaki Ghosh, Rupesh Shah, Parth Goyal, and Hemant for their efforts that helped fine-tune and shape my book to perfection. I want to offer sincere thanks to all and their team who helped make this happen.

- Thanks to all the people who have deep influence and have inspired me so much for imparting the immense wealth of knowledge, and enriching and widening my horizons.

- I am grateful to all my mentors, coaches, and spiritual gurus for their teachings and their incessant support in my life.

Lastly, I offer my sincere thanks to all the readers of this book. It is because of you that I have had the opportunity to pen down my experiences and learning, and turn it into a book. I hope you enjoy my humble attempt to pass on the knowledge that was given to me by my teachers, mentors and gurus.

Preface

The text contains ideas on how to seek happiness in more ways than one. It confirms the search for happiness. This is where self-image, decisions, education, analysis, behaviour, beliefs, and understanding come together to allow us to experience happiness. At its core, it's about self-confidence and acceptance. Spirituality means being true to ourselves, not doing something or being someone else. This thought is reflected in the book in the form of a collection of personal experiences. Many of these situations will be familiar to you and will bring to light the human differences that have kept us enslaved for a long time.

It aims to influence the reader and bring him to the light, towards self-control. Happiness is a process and cannot be achieved by simply trying it. This book reaches the minds of teenagers and helps them reach their essence and become a better version of themselves. It contains ideas and ways to improve self-control and emotions. Once a teenager knows how to properly handle emotions, they will be less likely to have confused thoughts. It's about our emotions, characters, and desires, and how we feel about ourselves.

When we learn more about ourselves, we can better accept and strengthen our weaknesses and insecurities.

Author's Note

If I had to briefly tell you what this book is about, I would say that it is my experience and I am learning it every day. This will also help you achieve happiness. So why did I choose to cover this particular topic in my book?

Well, there are a few reasons that ultimately led me to write this book, but what are at the top of the list are youth or teenagers of today. What worries me in particular is how these young people are currently leading their lives. They have created a misconception of the word "happiness." They believe that signing up for social media platforms and getting a large number of likes, followers, or retweets forms the basis for staying connected and experiencing happiness. Well, it's kind of a connection. It is the happiness of the external materialistic world. In other words, it is quite weak and boring; it is temporary. They posted on Instagram; some people liked it and even commented, praised or congratulated them. It feels great, but how long? Little by little, the attention shifts to the next person or post and they will not get any more acceptances now. That's it, happiness ends here. Why establish a connection transmitted by someone else's time, words, or actions? It's our luck, why do others have to decide this for us?

I'll give you another example. Let's say there is this new brand that launched a new bag. You always liked those things. Go get the bag. You feel great for a few days, combine the bag with a great outfit and take it with you every time you go out. People praise the bag, "Thank you very much! I got it from this brand, you know? After few days the bag loses all the exposure. It is no longer new, it is now common. A few more days will pass and the skin on this bag will start to wear away. That's the end of all the attention you would have gotten from a new bag. In this situation, too your feeling of happiness is related to the purchase of the bag. Therefore, you have no control over how long your happiness lasts, as it is always at a risk of falling. Once again, your happiness is determined by people or some object that you own.

This book will help young people to get all the answers about happiness and change their focus, so that they understand that life is more than this short-lived happiness.

1. Introduction to Happiness

Happiness is not a word that seems different to us; we have all heard it before. In fact, we all have more or less a clear idea regarding the same. This tends to differ from one person to another. For example, one could only need food to find happiness, whereas another person could only find happiness in dancing. Happiness has different meanings to all of us. Despite the medium being different, happiness hasn't failed to reach any of us. It would be rather wise to not try to capture the vast definitions of happiness in a single word. When babies are born, the doctors slap their back, so they can have their first cry. There is a perfectly fine explanation for the same; when the baby cries for the first time; its lungs expand, preparing it to be a functional organ of system. We aren't taught to cry in order to express our sadness, and the moment we experience it, we know what to do.

Similarly, happiness is an emotion that we are introduced to at the very beginning of life. It is fundamental because nobody teaches us to be happy. It is not only humans who experience this particular feeling. Every living creature has its own way of expressing its happiness. We smile, laugh, and sometimes even drop a tear or two when we are happy whereas dogs wave their tail or lick us to express their emotions. In that way, we can say, happiness has reached everybody in one way or another.

We can only share how we feel while we process this sense of happiness but can never really manage to capture the true essence of happiness in words. There is a valid reason for this; happiness tends to unfold specific explanations for specific people. If we ask a person to recall the time when they were happy, we will relate with the description of the feeling that they will provide. We will fail to find meaning in the source that brought them that happiness.

Let us inquire a little deeper into this matter. When we grow up, we tend to catch on the attitude and habits that the people around us display. This eventually tends to play a grand role in shaping our overall personality. These experiences are stored in our brains in the form of memories. There is a section in our brain that is categorised as injury. It is nothing but a kind of damage that our mind suffers from; it usually happens as an impact of a painful event. These injuries come back to us if we are set off by certain triggers. These encounters become even more alarming for people suffering from mental illnesses.

Happiness works in a similar way. Instead of distress, the events are joyful. But happiness also comes with its triggers. Let's call them 'Happiness triggers.'

Suppose, a child enjoys a little outing at the park and plays with his father every other day and as he grows up, his memory will take a very special place in his mind. Every time he goes near that park or talks about the park, his face will light up. He is just triggered by happiness.

HAPPINESS IS...

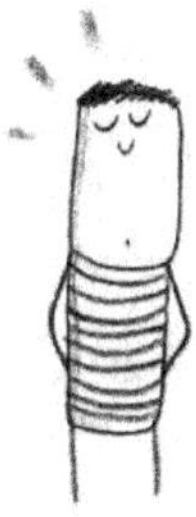

...being honest with yourself.

When we are kids, our thought process is rather simple. We are not burdened with the thought of earning a living, buying a house, and all the other thoughts that begin to accompany us as we slowly grow up. All we had to focus on was what made us happy. When we were kids, we weren't exposed to the wide rainbow of emotions. We knew that we had to cry when we were hurt, sad, or needed attention. However, one thing that we were never confused about was what brought us happiness. We laughed when we were happy, be it a toy, a person, or any simple activity that appeared as amazing to us. Kids are innocent because neither do they have the capacity to digest the vast knowledge of the world nor do they have any experience regarding the same.

Anyway, as we begin to grow up, we seem to get a hint of the different ways of the world. As we get more involved in the outer world, we focus less on ourselves and what brings us happiness. This is where we become sensitive. We lose control over ourselves, our emotions or our happiness. This is how our happiness becomes very weak. It can be snatched away very easily. In today's time, all it can take for us to stop smiling is a random phone call. Yes, that is how delicate the state of our happiness has become. We have forgotten to look within for happiness; we look for external factors to make us happy. That also explains why our happiness is so short-lived and unstable.

2. Where Do We Start?

When we talk about pleasure, there's a lot that comes to mind. But is there a way to know how to reach happiness? If we have to worry about formulas, we are definitely going to be upset. There will be a number of occasions in our lives that we feel like there is no turning back and no satisfaction. Please, do not feel that way, it will kill our will to do better and regain our happiness. If we see the smallest sign going our way, hang on to it. Does not hold back, take deep breaths, and calm down. Have faith in the power that controls and looks after us all. It will always help us in troubled times. Just do not lose faith because once we lose that, we are bound to feel helplessness and anxiety. Happiness becomes a doubtful idea at that point. We hardly know the amount of love that God has for us, and he is the creator of all, he will help us get through tough times easily, only if we keep our faith in him strong. We cannot let our faith shake even for a second. Doubt in god and faith arise from self-doubt. Happiness comes to us in various ways, only we have to be awake to see it. The answers to all our worries and problems lie in the sacred ancient texts. *Bhagavad Gita* is one of them. Lord Krishna says,

'When doubt enters the heart of an individual, he is totally lost, and he becomes miserable.'

These texts teach us lessons that are frequently overlooked in our today's lives. Look out for the positive, that's when we are going to be able to see better, and reach out to the satisfaction we deserve. It is necessary to be happy in life for survival. We are not always in contact with our true selves, and thus do not know what makes us genuinely happy. A lot of people do not know what it would be like to be happy with our lives. We have been misguiding from that direction, the path of compassion, the path of happiness. Maybe, we are looking at it differently, or we are taught to do so. Kids grow up taking reference of their world into account; we are no exceptions. Try to think of all the moments when we feel powerless or even broken. Does it hurt? Do we feel scared?

Do we never want to go back again to this particular memory ever again? If the answer is yes, then we are humans, and feeling this way is natural.

Our mind is a complicated web, a web so deep and complexly built that we do not have access to it all! The trick to being happy is to continue to feel it at all times even though we do not feel it, even though it feels terrible. Just do it. If we remain disappointed with everything in life, the light will never shine upon us. It doesn't take a lot of time to be happy, it's just the little things that help us get there, and the best part is, we are not even going to know that we are getting closer to happiness every day. No matter what sort of work we do; we have to put our heart and soul into it. We must assure ourselves that we should be content with that. We've got to keep doing this before we feel better. We know it's better said than done, but there's nothing to stop us from achieving our satisfaction. No matter what we do, do it with a smile, and do it happily. Most of the way, it's going to be difficult, not easy, so we've got to keep going. There's going to be a moment when we will stop feeling like we are pushing ourselves to feel this way. It would all seem normal since happiness is a part of us. That's the target. Consider joy an inseparable part of us, almost as normal as breathing. It's meant to come to us easily. But, in order to achieve that point, we must overcome our shyness. He who hesitates cannot get a new viewpoint. Being mindful of our frustration or unhappiness is central to the healing process.

Healing is not a one-step process. It requires utmost sincerity and determination. If we are not able to get awareness on both of these, we will not be able to do this. This does not mean that we cannot have complaints; we will and we should, because that is human. However, what matters is how we convey our concerns or unhappiness; our ways of expression. As we mentioned earlier, it is important that we become expressive because holding back has never done anyone any good. When we feel hurt, know that there are different ways to express or say it. We must do it with a smile on our face, and if a smile seems too much, at least be patient while talking. We must let the person know how exactly we feel about their actions, and that it has hurt us, instead of using harsh words and targeting hate towards them. We must say everything very calmly and try to be our best selves. Life is not as complicated as we think it to be. Life will put many hurdles in our way but our entity lies in how we deal with it. Show the world what we are made of. We are strong, stronger than we know. We often do not realise the amount of strength that we carry within ourselves. Find it and focus on it. A lot of individuals may feel affected by the hurdles in their way but the only thing that would do, is shake our faith. If we are able to hold our faith right in its place, we are winners. We should remain untouched by our surroundings and hold onto our faith in the power that protects us all. This will help us retain our energy and mental health because when times get rough, the first thing that runs out is our energy, and eventually we become unable to manage real life events.

> *There are two ways of looking at life. One is where we say, 'I will be happy after achieving a certain objective'. The latter being, 'I am happy, come what may!' Which one of these do we want to follow?*

Desires and wishes are different. Though they might be quite similar, they are never the same. We are all puppets of our destiny, but the least we can do is try to take charge of our lives. We wish for a lot of things, materialistic or not, but we do. Wishes are what bring us joy. We think that if we get them, everything would be great. Desires are slightly different from wishes. We think we need them to an extent that it becomes a necessity, something that we insist on having or owning. That is a very unhealthy practice and state of mind. In this situation, the lines between reality and imagination get blurred. The mind has a lot to do with each feeling, and especially these ones. Only a calm and quiet mind can pull through such strong emotions and rise as peaceful. The first thing that strong desires do to our minds is that they create chaos, so much chaos that we cannot even hear our own voice. We must not engage in any such thoughts. A peaceful mind has the power to reach out to God, to create some form of connection with him because we all know that to reach out to God would in some way mean bliss. We are no longer going to be blocked within our heads. A deep sense of peace will settle around us, the kind that helps us to breathe with ease, to laugh, to smile, even in pain, and to let the pain go beautifully. We enter a point where our happiness appears unhurt and untouchable by some external causes or stimulations. Nothing can cause hurdles in our joyful moments; finally, we are in control. And as we move forward on this definite path, we will finally satisfy our wishes and desires. The force that saves all of us will make a lot of things happen; we just have to give it some time. Patience is the answer, and as some suggest, the strength of patience is incomparable. If destiny rules us; we have a few things in our possession. We can't change destiny; however, we can shift it in the way we choose. We can change it. If we wait, our wishes will be fulfilled one way or the other, but if we are impatient, it can do us more harm than we know or can think of.

Our feelings are part of being human and there will be moments in our life when the best of us will get experience the ultimate. A circumstance can make us feel saddened. We might feel anger towards others. A certain circumstance could make us feel nervous. There are aspects of life that are natural. However, it is important for personal growth and development to let go of such negative emotions. To rid ourselves of toxins and to live a happy life, cleansing our minds is necessary.

Certain works of art are very similar, such as painting, writing, and gardening or playing, they enable the powers and energies beyond anything. One should rely on our artistic side to rest emotionally and rejuvenates. Mindfulness is the awareness at the moment. We seem to lose connection with the tense of the moment. Our minds are roaming. We are speaking about future or past concerns. Have we ever walked or driven for a period of time only to understand that we recall almost nothing of the trip upon arrival at the destination?

The ride does matter. What takes us to our final objective is the journey. We must learn how to enjoy this trip and only live in present. The end target would feel so much better. Mindfulness requires exercise.

It is a perfect way to practice mindfulness. Putting away our mobile devices is another way to be conscious and present at the moment. When catching up with friends or family, keeping the phone in our pockets or aside is a good idea.

We must bring full attention to the moment. It can also help to set our plans or objectives for the day first thing in the morning. This gives us attention and prepares us for the day. Slow down. We are constantly on the go in today's society. Spending time with loved ones can heal us in many ways.

Conflicts must be gone. We have to be conscious; it goes hand in hand with letting go of grievances. Let the anger go. Let the past go. The past is something that cannot be changed. Always look ahead and be confident about the future. Not every relationship or friendship, sadly, is intended to last. Take a step further for we must alter it if we are no longer content with any aspect of our lives. We are in the driver's seat and we must take it seriously. Book a flight if we want adventure. Feed our spirits. It is necessary to liberate ourselves, cleanse our life from negativity and toxicity, free our souls, and find our joy. Just remember, our time is right here, right now.

Once, a girl used to live with her parents until they decided to separate. After their separation, the girl felt as if her world had turned upside down. She hardly had the courage to accept what was going on in her life. They were a very happy family until that point, in her eyes. There was nothing more that she could ask for. She had grown up there and had turned out to be a very happy kid. This decision made her feel like her entire life was falling apart. A few months later, she shifted to her grandparent's house. She became quieter, wrapped herself up in her blankets every night, and cried herself to sleep. However, after a few months of trying, her grandparents could finally make her feel a bit normal and comfortable. She soon realised that her happiness had been in her own hands all this while. Pain will always disrupt our lives but what matters is if we let it stop us entirely. Suffering always remains optional, and so, she found happiness in her new life again.

Another way of feeling at peace with ourselves is the connection with God, and it can only be achieved if we open our hearts and let him reside there. We need to have an open mind and heart. If we keep closing ourselves to emotions, it would do us no good.

It's easy to get covered up in daily life and never take the time to think about the things we've done. In our lives, each of us has done plenty of cool things. So, what if at this very moment, life is not perfect? It's all right if our goals take a bit longer. Do not fear that we have not yet hit the height of our career.

The most important thing is that we are going forward and today, we are in a better place than yesterday. One amazing thing that helps to walk towards a better and happy future is developing different habits.

While there are millions and millions of hobbies in the world, each of them does not work for every individual. Nevertheless, there are a few hobbies that can work wonders in case of every other person.

Cooking

Cooking is one of the most interesting activities out there which everybody should try testing their hand at. Cooking enables us to be in the moment, entirely focused on the goods and processes at hand. It encourages us to think ahead too.

Painting

Painting may not appear to be a very fruitful hobby but it may give us some fantastic insight on our lives, and help us to unlock our artistic side.

Painting helps us to dig deep into our mind's emotions which can help us transform them into something great.

It could also motivate us to be more creative at other aspects of our life.

Writing

One of the most productive hobbies we can turn to is writing in our free time. Writing is an extremely strong and an essential mean of self-expression. It can help us channel our emotions into something that we feel passionate about, and through which we can discharge our feelings, wishes, and desires.

Writing posts, novels, radio scripts or diary entries helps us in unleashing our artistic side.

Gardening

Is there something more profoundly calming than gardening, at least in theory?

Gardening is not only a fun and enjoyable pastime; it's also a perfect way to improve us.

How is that?

Gardening helps us to rest by saving our energies for the busy days ahead of us. Managing or taking care of plants also prepares us for handling others tasks.

As we all know, plants need a lot of care, especially in their initial days. Thus, adopting a plant can be as good as adopting a pet. Therefore, it encourages us to devote a significant piece of our time as well as our energy. Similar to cooking, painting and writing, gardening can be extremely soothing to our minds.

Helping out in the household

While painting, reading and writing does involve us in engaging any physical activities, participating in the household assignment will.

Helping out our mother or siblings, and taking a little work off their plate will not only do them good but will also be freeing to us. Cleaning up our room sounds like it would be a lot of work and makes us run as away from it as fast as we can. In reality, performing assignments like cleaning up our rooms or washing our own clothes gives us a sense of fulfilment.

Along with a sense of fulfilment, we develop a feeling of independence which is a way for happiness.

We clear up our minds only for happiness to make its way in. We remove all the unnecessary thoughts that make us uneasy and replace it with a positive feeling.

...choosing your own path.

'All work and no play makes Jack a dull boy.'

It is one of the most used proverbs which can be interpreted as-'Without any leisure from work, a person could become unproductive'.

It is sad that a lot of teachers stress students to focus in the majority of their time, and only play if there's any time left in their tight schedule.

It is as important for a child to take some time out for themselves as much as it is to spend on assignments such as studying.

People move from their phase of a child to an adult without any memories of playing around or spending time playfully. They likely miss out on the basic elements of a childhood and consequently, they miss out on the happiness it could have brought them.

This is why all the children as well as adults must be as invested in their studies or work as much as they should be in playing or taking time off.

We've heard the saying, 'It's the little things that matter in life'. The little things that really make us happy are small and sometimes unnoticed aspects of life. We must make our lives revolve around the things that truly make us happy; and enjoying what we do is the only way to do great work. Keep searching even if we haven't found it yet. We will know when we find it, as we do in all matters of the heart. People who do what they enjoy are likely to live a happier and more prosperous life, have greater self-esteem, and better health. Coming to searching for God within ourselves, we can reach God if we are clear-headed with a kind heart as he resides right here, in us. We only fail to see it because we are too engaged in other things and other complications of life that we feel as barriers. Cleansing our hearts and souls is the only way to reach our inner self, and eventually, happiness.

There are a few questions that we need to ask ourselves in order to understand how far we have come and how far we want to reach in our life. Are we really satisfied with what we have or do we want more? There are a plenty of questions that can shake us up from inside if not answered properly. What we do is, we often do not think about these things. We do not put enough effort about these issues, because if we do, we feel like our head is going to burst with all the pressure, unanswered questions, and fear. The absolute thought of search deeper into our personality feels like aggression, let alone anybody else doing it. Here is how we can help ourselves to turn around our days and be content, or at least try a bit.

- We can start with telling ourselves that we are fine the way we are.

- We can achieve whatever we want to if we try enough.

There is no alternative to honesty, good intention, and hard work. Being with people who are making us happy is important. Studies indicate that when we are with people who are also happy, we are happiest. Stick with the cheerful ones and let them rub off on us.

Keeping hold of our beliefs, what we find real, what we know is equal, and all the values we believe in. The more we honour them over time, the better we feel about ourselves and everyone we love.

Accept what's fine. We must look at our life, take a look at what works, and not, drive anything away just because it's not perfect.

If good things happen, let them in, even the very little ones.

Imagine what's best. Do not be afraid to look and see ourselves getting what we really want. Many people avoid this method because if things do not work out, they do not want to be frustrated. The reality is that it plays a huge role because imagining what we want makes us act to achieve it.

Do the things that we love. We may not be able to take a holiday every season, but as long as we get to do the things, we enjoy every once in a while, we are going to find more of the happiness we deserve,

Those who think they are contributing to humanity's well-being appear to feel better about their lives. Many people simply do it because it's rewarding, and they want to be part of something greater than they are.

Listening to our hearts and minds equally is crucial. The only one that fills us up is us. Our family and friends may think that we would be great at something. Following our bliss can be difficult. Just be clever, and for the time being, keep the day job.

It's attractive to believe that our fulfilment is the duty of someone else, but the fact is that it's really our charge. We have the strength to get to where we want to go until we know that. Avoid blaming others, God or the universe, and much sooner we will find our answers.

To alter, be available. Even if it doesn't feel good, the one thing we can count on is improvement. Change will occur, so make emergency arrangements and actions for the experience emotionally.

'Those who love you, treasured memories, silly jokes, warm days, and starry nights—these are the ties that bind and the gifts that keep on giving.'

Happiness and satisfaction are within our control, but only out of reach sometimes. The first step to finding them more frequently is to know what works best for us.

People talk a lot about seeking happiness as if happiness is something we can ride on in the street. This does not put us in the seat of the driver. What if we changed our outlook to think of happiness as something we fulfil, instead of hoping, dreaming, and praying that one day, we will wake up to find happiness staring us right in the face? What if happiness, rather than something that just happens to us is all about what we do in our lives?

The variables to happiness appear more or less out of our understanding when we frame happiness as just an emotion. Again, this puts us completely out of the driver's seat.

But if we reframe and begin to think of happiness as a skill, in fact, the most valuable skill in life, we make greater walks in our lives to achievements.

There are three particular points we can follow that will ignore any negative feeling or negative energy around us.

- Let individuals know that we care.

- Create time for individuals.

- Avoid engaging with negative people and make more space for people who make us feel good about ourselves.

...thinking about what you're
grateful for.

Why does this work?

Since feeling is linked to our hearts whether we are shy or friendly, whether we are having a great day or a bad day, it is something that we all desperately need and want in our lives. We feel more connected to our culture and ultimately ourselves by reaching out.

3. Difficulty on Our Way to Happiness

Let's try to understand this with the help of an example.

There used to live this woman who was affected with sadness. Her mental torture had reached out to her physical health and had begun damaging it as well. She used to be depressed all day and complained about experiencing pain all over her body. Tired with all her complaints, her husband went to a doctor. Surprisingly, all the tests that the doctor had suggested came out to be normal. The doctor put out his final verdict-'There is nothing wrong with her. She needs a little bit of shopping. Retail therapy will completely fix her.'

This statement took them by shock. We tend to confuse what it feels to keep ourselves happy and entertain others. We try to be happy in hopes that maybe we will find happiness in the process. Activities such as shopping might be able to keep our mind away for some time but it will never be successful in finding ultimate happiness. We cannot be happy until we know what is not letting us be happy. Unless we truly understand what our consciousness stands for, we cannot find happiness.

There is a famous saying that goes by the lines of - 'To truly learn something, we have to unlearn it first.'

It's a very popular line used by teachers around the world. Let's take an example of any subject. In lower standards, such as sixth or seventh, students are offered only a partial understanding of what the subject is. Students simply do not understand the definitions until they are offered with a higher degree. However, if they have the partial knowledge that they have acquired from the subject while learning about it, it may become difficult for them to understand. Growing up, they would know that though some ideas turned out to be false, it was necessary for them to understand them in order to get a better understanding of the definition.

Whether its physics, mathematics or geography, we know all about how we progress. When we are children, our minds do not have the ability to digest conceptual ideas. For us, then, the same concepts are shortened so that we can understand the basic elements of the subject. When we move towards higher expectations, we are introduced with an initial powerful definition that may also be opposite to the one we learned earlier. It is also very important to unlearn until we practice again. To unlearn, we need to recall what we've known, and then, personally, abolish it. We will only think again if we have a blank mind with no fixed thoughts of the same kind.

The process of finding happiness can be similar.

- We have to have a clear idea of what the true nature of our awareness is.

- We have to stop postponing our happiness in the name of 'working towards happiness'.

- We need to turn away from all the false ideas of happiness or finding happiness we had in our mind.

Only after we tick each of these, can we be set on the true path to achieving the ultimate happiness.

HAPPINESS IS...

...a celebration.

All these instructions might make one feel like that happiness is nothing but a skill that one has to develop with time. But that is not true. As mentioned at the very beginning, the term 'happiness' is explained in different ways by different people. When we look at the word 'happiness', we are reminded of the last time when we were happy or the people who make us happy. Do we ever look at the word and think that I am happy now? No, we do not.

We were brought up to think that joy was covered up in memories. We are trying to catch happiness in a package so that we can still have it with us and enjoy it anytime we want to. Today, not only do we want to catch pleasure in our hearts, but we still want to freeze the moment in images. Instead of loving the moment, we are taking pictures of everything with our phones or cameras. Now, the funny thing is that in the future, when we are going to remember the experience by looking at the photo, we are never going to be able to get back the fun we experienced at that time.

We are wasting time by holding our memories. In the end, we cannot know what it must have been like to have existed in the moment, to have truly welcomed the happiness.

We have a false view of happiness in our minds which decides that we can save happiness later on. We also define happiness as an experience in the future, though happiness can only be practised today.

We look at happiness as if it's money, we save it for a later day, for a more meaningful case, and for a happier day. We can't accept money being the right comparison to happiness – never has it been, never can it be. If anything, happiness is like time. We cannot store time for the future. What is meant for the present has to be lived, enjoyed, and spent in the present; future is not a place where we can push the present to.

Happiness is now.

> '*We postpone our happiness until some perfect day in the future, but it never arrives. It's like making a bed all night but having no time to sleep. Creation wants to see us happy, yet we keep on postponing our happiness.*'

In Sanskrit, there is a word called *Ekant*. In Hindi, it will translate to 'loneliness' but in Sanskrit, it means 'the end of loneliness'. There is no parallel found to this word in any other language.

On the surface, loneliness may mean the absence of a company. However, if we really explore the origins of the term, we will realize that loneliness simply means being separated from our inner self. We may be in a crowd and yet feel alone and sad. On the other side, we will be happy and single.

In the end, it's all in our control. Like pleasure, we can opt not to be alone. We've got to relate to our inner self. As soon as we get clarification about our inner self, we take full control of ourselves.

There was a very famous comedian from America called Robin Williams. Even today, he is considered to be one of the best comedians till date. Now, of all the jobs in the world, he chose to be a comedian. If we were to understand the job of a comedian in a few sentences, then it would literally mean 'to spread happiness'. A comedian cracks jokes and makes people laugh.

How can a person who has literally taken up the profession of making a person happy not be happy himself?

Seems odd, doesn't it? It is quite saddening and unexpected, but at the same time, it is the truth.

He got so affected with the sadness that it took over him, and in the end, he gave in. He left us; he left the world very soon. He had fame, he had money, he had everything one could ask for, and yet he was not happy. Despite having the world as his audience, he was not happy.

He decided to make the world happy, make them laugh, but there was nothing that could make the stop hurting entirely.

The only way we can deal with this is with spiritual practice. Spiritual practice is a kind of learning through which we can reach a higher degree of calm and access our true self. It includes the simple method of meditation, which allows one to take slow deep breaths, but also requires the participation of a few other items. We are going to list each step so that it's easier to learn about it.

Other than reflection, it's a perfect way to focus on our emotions and let go of all the problems held up.

Here it goes:

Meditation has worked wonders for people suffering from insomnia as well. It calms our mind, and our system removes every element that could possibly cause us anxiety.

However, while practising meditation, we have to remember that our goal is to relax the distressed mind and not to put it to sleep.

We can sit in the position of Sukhasana, Vajrasana, or the Padmasana. There are no strict rules regarding the position except keeping the back straight.

If we sit or stand in the wrong position, the entirety of the breath that we inhale does not reach our brain. Thus, instead of making us feel calm, light, and fresh, it makes us lazy, tired, and sleepy.

Let go

On a regular busy day of our lives, we know what we have to do throughout the day. Our thought process requires us to think about certain things in order to execute.

We hardly ever get any time for ourselves. We are always so busy with our schedule that we forget to stop and experience the moment. Meditation asks us to let go of all these thoughts and routines. Whenever we are busy or stressed, our eyebrows or our backs get tensed.

While meditating, we have to let go of all the stress that is the result of a busy life in the city. We have to entirely let go.

In meditation, we do not have a plan. We have to let the process take its original and natural course. We have to keep ourselves from interrupting and taking a different course from the natural one.

All these thoughts must not appear as instructions to us. These are just suggestions that will help us achieve clarity.

Acknowledge the thoughts

Our minds never stop functioning. We can access only the conscious part of our minds when we are awake, but our minds never stop. Like the other organs of our body, our minds keep working even while we sleep. We go to sleep with a mind full of thoughts and wake up with a mind full of thoughts.

Thus, whatever we do, our mind will keep creating thoughts. While meditating, our job will be to not take part in these thoughts. We have to observe them without changing them or putting our additions to them. We have to observe as an outside entity, and not try to participate in it. Since our habit is to invest in the thought process, it will be a real challenge for us to just reflect without engaging.

Practice Prayer or Chanting

We have been asked many times to not engage in the natural flow of our thought process. Fixating on a particular prayer can come off as a conflict to what has been stated in the earlier. It is important that we do not block the natural flow of the process, but we can choose a particular prayer, and try to focus on that while our thought process acts out in the background. Not only is it known to develop our concentration power but it also nurtures our ability to remember.

Now, it is not necessary for us to pick a religious prayer. It can be anything from a motto to a sentence that makes us feel safe or empowered. It depends entirely on ourselves since the process is concentrated on freeing us of any negative thought that unnecessarily stresses us.

Reflect on the thoughts

Feel it, and enjoy the lightness our body feels. We have to think about the entire process and how we went about it. We have to notice how we have become less disturbed than before the meditation. We have to accept that our reaction to the process was natural.

We have to turn our focus to our body and our space attention and appearance. We have to become aware of the climate. We have to observe what our body feels, be attentive to our breathing and emotions and stay fully relaxed and calm. Then, we will slowly open our eyes and sit for some time in the same place. We must let the meditation's effects sink in.

4. Pain and Suffering

Every day we think about how we want our lives to be created. Each day will be special and will make us feel better. When that doesn't happen, we lose sight of who we are, and we feel incapable. Even if one is unable to work properly, think straight, and so much more. We will start to fail, but we won't stop. It feels like no one is out there to stop this pain and make us feel better. In a case like this, meditation will work well for us. We always fail to understand how we end up hurting more than we could ever imagine. Life brings us suffering, but if we wish to suffer, it is upon us. There is always a choice which we can make; a conscious choice. As humans, we have the power, our intelligence, and the freedom to deal with ourselves in any way we want. To our advantage, we must learn how to use it. Life would make us face discouragement that could lead us to give up as we have no proper method to win over it. Meditation and *pranayama* work for our souls, not just the bodies. Practice and patience make us what we are, and over the years, we will get a better understanding of how to deal with pain and suffering.

An experience that brings us to the depths of who we are is meditation. Up to that point in our life, we, as ourselves, have stripped ourselves of all the confusions we had about ourselves. We feel joy and happiness in the process. Our being is warmed up by a sense of love and light. Meditation helps us to understand the universal reality and to let go of all that has happened and is going to happen. The present is where we want to be and where we want to find peace and comfort. Here is how we can lead ourselves to less suffering through meditation. These simple steps can go a long way.

Meditation is considered to be the seventh arm of the eight-fold path of yoga. Meditation may be an ancient ritual, but it is practised to establish a sense of relaxation and inner harmony in cultures all over the world. While the practice has links to many different religious teachings, meditation is less about faith and more about altering consciousness, seeking awareness, and experiencing peace.

Breathing Emphasis

The emphasis on breathing is one of the simplest meditation methods for anxiety and stress. We sit quietly and breathe in and out slowly. Pay attention to the flow of air going in and out of our body, taking note of the sensations that occur when we inhale and exhale. Count from 1 to 10, with each following inhale, thinking of each number.

Pranayama

It is not necessarily meditation, but it is used most often as meditation preparation. It consists of concentrating the mind through breathing that is controlled. Breathing into a number of 4, holding for a number of 4, breathing out to a number of 4, and holding again for a number of 4 is the most common *pranayama* technique. This is an outstanding anxiety meditation technique on its own.

We should use positive affirmations in our meditation. It is especially helpful for anxiety because affirmations remind us that we are good individuals, deserving of love and acceptance. This also leads us to a more positive viewpoint of others and the world. We should use breath and silence along with statements about ourselves, others, and the world to increase our positive feelings and reduce our feelings of mistrust and insecurity.

These are a few helpful techniques:

Ujjayi

Ocean Breath (*Ujjayi Pranayama*) is most widely used to support yoga postures. In this breathing procedure, we concentrate on the back of our throat to support the extension of each breathing period. Each inhale and exhale is long, total, and deep. We must practice this breath when sitting in a relaxed cross-legged position. Once we get the hang of it, we can start using it during our yoga session.

Bhastrika

When we perform some physical activity, our body needs more blood, which signals the heart to pump harder, thereby increasing the heartbeat. One unique aspect of *Bhastrika Pranayama* is that we produce more oxygen without the body calling for it. *Bhastrika Pranayama* is a method of quick inhale and exhale, which provides a lift to the body and is also referred to as the yogic breath of fire.

Anulom Vilom

Anulom Vilom Pranayama is a common breathing technique associated with conventional yoga that is used to relax the mind and body. *Anulom* can be interpreted as 'with grain' or 'natural' while *vilom* means 'against grain.' We will do this exercise by deep breathing and exhalation, switching between the right and the left nose with the aid of our fingertips.

Kapalbhati

Kapalbhati Pranayama consists of short, strong exhalations and quiet inhalations. This exercise is a traditional purification procedure or *kriya* that balances and filters the respiratory system by enabling the release of waste and toxins. It serves as a tonic for the system, cleansing, and revitalizing the body and mind.

Breathing while chanting OM (Udgeeth Pranayama)

Udgeeth Pranayama is the simplest and most popular pranayama of all. Being given the name of 'breathing exercise', it is nothing if not the art of conscious breathing. What it takes might be a little commitment of our time on a regular basis to experience the wonderful benefits that *pranayama* can provide us with. *Udgeeth Pranayama* requires basic hearing vibrations that echo and awaken the consciousness to its built-in, infinite capacity. Thinking, being awake, and alert to its ability, is capable of understanding.

It is, therefore, necessary to concentrate exclusively on the stated implications in the *pranayama* follow-up. *Udgeeth Pranayama* is effective at treating depression, insomnia, loss of attention, and other disorders linked to the brain. *Udgeeth Pranayama* involves the singing of AUM (OM) for every exhalation – that can last up to twenty seconds.

Chanting Meditation

Our ancient sages recognized some unique sound waves that carry the mind to a state of calmness and harmony in addition to providing other benefits. Those sounds are considered mantras. They cause the mind to dissolve and to recover. These small, positive vibrations often establish the zone of positivity in us.

Bhanu Maa quite rightly explained: The sound of someone crying can make us feel sad, while the sound of someone smiling can give us a sense of laughter. When the sounds of crying and laughter will affect us so much, the mantras are much more powerful and help us step smoothly through the inner, quiet room.

There is a certain saying in Sanskrit: *Mananat Trayate Iti mantrah* (मननात् त्रायते इति मन्त्रः॥). It says that mantra is the one that protects us from repeating. Look closely; we are so concerned about everything in life, but what exactly is it that we are worried about? It's nothing but a constant feeling about something in the past or uncertainty about the future. And our mind continues to roll around between the past actions and future events and is caught up in an overflow of worry.

Mantras come to support, save us from constant chaos, and help bring our thoughts to the present moment. It is then that we enjoy a deep sense of meditation.

Chanting mantras charge the environment with optimistic vibrations, and such an ambiance lets meditation become normal and effortless.

Meditation with Music

Music has many great effects on the control of depression and mental wellness. It can help us quiet down our physiology without making much effort, and it can remove tension from our minds. Music can boost our mood, slow down our breathing, and trigger other stress-reducing improvements as well.

Meditation is also for a good cause, one of the most common stress control strategies—it offers short-term advantages, including a relaxed mind and body, and helps build immunity over time. Combining music with meditation will deepen the positive benefits and minimise our tension.

When we say music, it reminds different people of different tunes. A person can find comfort in Sufi while the other finds peace in rock music. However, when we talk about meditation with music, we are specifically highlighting slow music that helps us move to a state of calm. Music spreads over a wide range of variety, from sounds of nature to tunes of instruments.

A lot of people find the sounds of rain, singing of birds, the sound of a river flowing, or the crashing of waves and prefer to listen to them while meditating or before go to sleep. On the other hand, instruments like sitar, bamboo, or flute also produce a certain melodious tune that helps us calm ourselves down in moments of restlessness.

Guided Meditation

It refers to a form of meditation where a teacher, guru, or instructor guides through the process.

When starting out, it is advised that we be guided by an expert along with the simple steps of our meditation practice. It's important to have an experienced teacher, whatever kind of ability we acquire in life, who we can trust and connect to. But when it comes to exploring the confusion and the fine distinction of the mind, it is not only important, it is essential.

Before we get started, we need to understand what we are trying to achieve through meditation. Our instructor may ask us to imagine a certain day in our lives that makes us happy or reach out to a personal memory that always brings us peace.

Body Scan meditation

We can be so covered up in our tension that we fail to realize that the physical distress we have been experiencing—such as headaches, back, shoulder pain, and strained muscles are from our mental state.

This meditation is a good way to relieve the anxiety that we do not even know we are feeling. Body scanning involves paying attention to areas of the body and their sensations in a slow manner from foot to head.

By mentally scanning ourselves, we bring consciousness to any aspect of our body, finding every tension or discomfort. The goal is not to fully relieve the discomfort, but to get to know it and learn from it so that we can handle it better.

Body scan meditation is associated with both emotional and physical health effects. Studies suggest that stress control is one of the key advantages of body scan meditation, which can have many physical benefits, including decreased inflammation, nausea, and insomnia.

Body scan meditation is a very helpful and effective meditation that can help us get back to a calm state when we get too nervous.

There are several different ways to learn meditation methods. In a yoga or meditation class, we can learn them. To see how it's handled, we can get a book on meditation or even watch a film. It is important to consult with a yogi or other meditation expert to make sure we are doing them correctly.

Having said that, it is also important to remember that the goal we aim to achieve is a state of peace while clearing our minds. We do not need to choose a difficult form of yoga or meditation to achieve our goal. Different approaches work for different people. Therefore, we have to work through the varieties to realize what brings us happiness and peace in the end.

The process can vary for different individuals but what remain constant is the determination, consistency, and commitment we devote towards the process. We have to select any particular time of the day and perform the activity. Just breathe and let go, and we won't be too far from our expected path.

We now have a better idea of how to perform yoga and activities. Mental exercises sit at the top of the list. The goal here is to prepare our minds, and meditation serves as a platform for it. Now that we know how to initiate the journey and follow it in certain ways, we need to know how it helps our mental health and brings us to happiness. Meditation or mindfulness helps us to calm down, promotes deeper reflection of ourselves, and can help us find positive aspects about ourselves.

- Meditation tends to improve self-awareness by raising the ability without judgment to decide one's thoughts and feelings, which ends up improving self-esteem.

- In meditation, repeating a mantra, such as a word or a phrase, may also have a soothing effect, and we can change our mind away from distracting thoughts by focusing on our mantra.

- Meditation helps train our mind to concentrate on the moment, making us less likely to think on depression-fuelled anxious thoughts.

- Meditation can help relieve stress and anxiety and should be part of a holistic strategy for mental health care.

- Meditation can assist those with anxiety to relax their minds and relieve depressive symptoms, including sleep issues, lack of appetite, and low mood.

- Another miraculous thing that meditation can do for us is to help us control physical pain. It might sound foolish, but it is not. There are going to be times when we feel physical pain, but we must not let it get to our heads. However, this does not mean that it can entirely make the pain go away, but it will ease out the pain a bit. It will help us mentally prepare to handle the pain.

Now, we can talk about how the misery that pain carries along with it can vanish. It is human nature to feel afraid or get affected by pain, but we have to refrain from getting shocked or affected. So, what we have to concentrate on is trying to improve the way we think. We may not be able to reprogram our brains, but we can definitely make alterations. On our road to managing pain and suffering, these small steps will go a long way. In some situations, changing our attitude works best. Many of us are worried about our lives and what's going on, but we can still work to get a stronger and clearer picture of ourselves. Viewpoint forms us into the individuals we are and that begins with the amount of influence we have over our minds.

Let's consider that in all aspects of our life, there is an entity that has frustrated us and has created problems. It caused us to be depressed, anxious, distracted, angry with others, dissatisfied with our lives, overweight, unhealthy, not exercising or eating well, and much more.

A horrible entity, isn't it? Imagine now that there was a medicine that could relieve this entity's bad effects, and make all those other places better.

The material is real and the pain is ours. We all suffer every day in small and large ways. All the other issues are caused by it.

Also, the issue is real, it is compassionate to us. That sounds too soft for most people, but in all aspects of our life, it's a real activity that can have concrete benefits.

Let's discuss pain for a minute, and what would happen if we were to apply the method of self-compassion.

If we lead normal lives, we do not always think of ourselves as suffering. But actually, more often than we generally know, we suffer from birth itself. We struggle in small ways, and that impacts our happiness during the day, the happiness of those around us, and our behaviour and habits.

- Stress: Things happen to irritate us throughout the day such as a new thing added to our workload or someone who blames us for not doing housework. This is discomfort, but it is typically at low levels (though sometimes it can get to high levels). This suffering will be reduced by self-compassion, which will encourage us to be more comfortable with these events or situations, increasing our level of satisfaction throughout the day.

- Frustrations: Minor frustrations happen all the time, from people who do not do it right to congested traffic to not being able to find out why software doesn't work right. There is a pain as well. Compassion will help us calm down the frustrations and manage situations better. If we replied, we would be less upset, which is likely to result in better results.

- Anger with others: Our kid just won't listen; our spouse said a cruel thing; obviously, we are suffering. This can contribute not only to unhappiness, but also to actions that hurt our friendship, our job, and our relationship with others. Instead, apply self-compassion, and we will calm down. Respond correctly, even with compassion for the other person who is suffering as well.

- Feeling bad about ourselves: From disappointment to body fat to hopelessness in bad circumstances, there are a million reasons we feel bad about ourselves. This too is pain, and it causes us to take unhealthy actions such as comforting ourselves, not taking actions, not trusting in ourselves, with food and shopping.

- Feeling pressured: There's always a feeling in our days that we need to speed up to the next thing. We are walking, we are going fast. Even while working, we constantly turn to the next task, next super-urgent-can't-wait-do-it-now task. This sense of extreme urgency is the source of tension itself. Self-compassion will also relieve this and allow one to calm down in order to appreciate the moment, to be content at every moment.

- Distraction: We live super-distracted lives, wasting most of our day. We get diverted because of anxiety, we are afraid of tougher tasks, of losing out, of failing, and we believe distraction is calming. Distraction is a sign of pain. We feel bad for ourselves; we delay important tasks and make our work and lives worse. Distraction appears to increase pain. Self-compassion allows one to see this pain, relieve it, and reduce the urge to distract ourselves.

- Hesitation: On the job, on the writing, on learning a musical instrument, on exercise, we all hesitate. Like diversion, hesitation is a symbol of pain, anxiety, and of thinking that we can't do anything. That pain and self-compassion will help minimize hesitation, improve our productivity, help us take care of activities, and all the stuff we feel we really want to do but do not do. More suffering can be caused by hesitation as a lack of exercise contributes to worse health, which leads to disease, stress, and pain. Self-compassion assists us to continue to exercise actively and joyfully.

- Unhealthy eating: Because we are scared of vegetables, we consume unhealthy junk food to relieve ourselves from other miseries, and because we feel the need to take support of temporary pleasures. Self-compassion relieves this pain and encourages us to not eat unhealthy food. It makes our bodies feel better and makes us feel okay.

- Lack of gratitude: Most of our days are spent in sorrow, or even not so silent. In our lives, we are so dissatisfied with little things, which is a form of discomfort. These complaints mean that what's amazing about our lives is losing out. Self-compassion allows us to manage the discomfort of these complaints, and instead turn to the amazing things for which we should be thankful, increasing our satisfaction with life all around us.

- Lack of awareness: Most of our lives are spent in confusion, unaware of the present moment. This is a form of suffering because we could stay in the present much of the time if we weren't suffering, fully appreciating the moment as it happens. Instead, we are thinking about the future because we are worried about it and we are obsessed with our past mistakes. Self-compassion can relieve these concerns and obsessions, and instead, practice mindfulness more often with each moment.

Because pain takes many forms, we could go on to talk about it forever. But we can see the pattern; self-compassion eases the pain of suffering, decreases the bad outcomes, and we can choose more helpful ways of living. When it comes to healing ourselves, self-compassion is essential. What makes us understanding ourselves is forgiving ourselves for our faults, taking life as it goes, and reflecting on what worries us. We have to try to motivate ourselves to get through the pain.

HAPPINESS IS...

...meditating.

- Firstly, noticing and observing that we are feeling unhappy is important. We must keep a check on ourselves. It might be funny, but as humans, we often fail to notice, something that is right in front of us. It will bring us closer to self, and help us understand ourselves better than before. It is likely that we will be surprised upon seeing or discovering new things about ourselves. Things that we had not noticed before.

- Feeling the pain stands crucial in our journey to no suffering. Suffering is an option; it always has been. We need not suffer every time we face a situation that does not favour us. Pain is supposed to be tiring for any individual, but to let it pass by is the trick.

- We must accept the presence of pain, and how it makes us feel instead of being in disapproval of it. Its presence is real, and we must face it. We must let ourselves do so in order to get over it. Feel every bit of the pain. Try to do the best that we can, and we will see the difference in some time.

5. Looking for Happiness in Peace

Happiness comes more easily when we feel good about ourselves without feeling the need for anyone else's approval. We function, we research, and we hope to get some happiness. If we earn, satisfaction depends on the accomplishment of our aims or on the availability of a work. Now, the question is, was it really meant to be like that? The fact is it wasn't that way. We've trained our minds to believe that happiness lies in external factors such as income, vehicle, jobs, etc. We have also trained our minds to believe that we will never be a source of happiness individually. That's why we set goals and make a list of things we are going to do while we tell we are ourselves that happiness is our inspiration.

Sucheta is a girl who has always wanted to be a doctor. She has been working hard to achieve her goal. She has put everything else in the back seat and devoted all of her, so she could focus entirely on her studies. She thought to herself that once she becomes a doctor, she can rest and enjoy all the little happy moments that life has to offer. Her parents and loved ones encouraged the same idea. In the meantime, she discarded all the habits or activities that would make her happy in order to become a doctor. She started devoting less time to herself and more time to her studies that she considered would bring her happiness. Now, this can ideally have two outcomes:

Due to some unavoidable circumstances, she could not pursue this degree, and she could not achieve her dream of becoming a doctor, or she gets her degree and becomes a successful doctor.

Let's see both of these outcomes but one by one. In the first scenario, Sucheta dedicated all of her into one particular aim of achieving her goal of becoming a doctor. She believed that everything would be all right once she became a doctor. What she did not take into consideration is the fact that her source of happiness is unreliable. She expected happiness to arrive along with the completion of her goal. Thus, when she failed to complete her goal, happiness failed to arrive as well. All these months where she denied herself any break or some time to simply enjoy her time would all feel worthless at this point?

Now, the second scenario, let's assume all has gone according to plan and Sucheta has been successful in achieving her dream; she is a successful doctor today. She is happy today. She is happy at this very moment, but will a moment's happiness be enough to keep her contended throughout her entire life? Suppose, something goes wrong tomorrow; will she still be happy recalling the fact that she ignored all the fun to become a doctor? She might be happy for a while but it will not be enough. Remember when we talked about the delicacy of happiness? The same scenario can come into play here as well. After a month or two, she can come across a disturbing event or hear of bad news, and all this happiness will take no time to vanish into thin air.

All of this happened because Sucheta considered an external factor responsible to provide her with happiness; she expected this external factor to be her honest source of happiness. That is exactly where she went wrong.

'A child thinks he will be happy once he goes to college. Once in college, he thinks he will be happy when he starts earning. Then he thinks he will be happy once he is married. And the story goes on but that special day never comes!'

We are not even for once suggesting that students should not work hard to reach their goals. We are here to support them and encourage them through their journey of earning a degree or choosing the kind of lifestyle they want to. What we want to shed light on is that while preparing for their future, children must not turn a blind eye to what is happening now; they must not lose sight of the present. The future is no doubt important but so is the present, if not more.

We have been told that success lies in the future, and we have to work for it. We then came up with the idea that in order to be successful in life, we need to have a career, we need to gain a decent degree, and we need to make a name for ourselves. These things could bring us pleasure but they're going to be short-lived. As soon as we let go of these or lose all of them, the pleasure attached to them will be gone as well. Our state of happiness depends very much on the nature of certain materials or accomplishments.

There are many people who are extremely rich and privileged, and have almost anything a person could ask for. But, at the end of the day, if anybody asks them if they are happy, they will hesitate to answer. They focussed so much on their business, job, or wealth that they lost track of what they were really after, the true state of happiness. They might own all this wealth, but they do not own their happiness. Thus, no matter how rich they are, they will be sad at the end of their day.

We can only access the true state of happiness once we focus on that very aspect, not on different external sources that promise to bring us happiness. The only way we can let go of this dependency is by taking the path to spirituality. It is the only thing that can truly teach us the true meaning of inner peace and the real state of happiness. If we are happy with ourselves, then no bad news can take it away from us.

Why?

The reality of our happiness is not conditional to anything else but ourselves. We are the true owner of our happiness and nobody can snatch it away from us.

It is important to earn a degree and have a job but that is not our primary source of happiness. We are the primary source of our happiness. We do not have to run after money and education to achieve happiness; we will comfortably achieve anything we want to because we are happy.

Spirituality tells us that happiness is present within. Our external conditions can't have any influence on our state of mind if we are happy from inside or if we have found our peace of mind. We can be going through a time of hopelessness or loneliness, but if we keep our minds stable, it will be easier to focus on our object.

We were born with humbleness and that is what we should hold on to. 'Ego' is a concept humans have manufactured for our pride. We have made ourselves believe that feeding the ego will do us good and make us happy whereas the truth is rather the opposite. If we stick to our humbleness and look within, we will rise with happiness.

Change is a very deadly element. Once our change is visible to others, they will be eager to explore the topic. They might even be inspired to change themselves.

And, thus, we will prove the saying right:

'BE THE CHANGE YOU WANT TO SEE IN THE WORLD.'

— Mahatma Gandhi

Popular experiences indicate that when bad things happen to people, some individuals stay positive, while some are full of worry and are upset even in the best of circumstances. In fact, amongst the people we meet, it is very easy to find two people roughly matched by age, income, occupation, and marital status, one of whom is often positive and fully charged, and the other is affected by doubts, dissatisfaction, and tension.

What explains the deeper, more lasting difference between individuals in happiness? Such difference does exist and are true. Happiness and well-being self-analysis are reasonably constant, even over periods of many years.

HAPPINESS IS...

...making peace with your past
so it won't mess up
your present.

Studies have compared individuals with stable living conditions to those going through major life changes, or those with increasing or declining incomes, and they still find that at the end of the research, the best sign of how happy people are is how happy they were at the start.

6. Are we Happy with Ourselves?

> *'It is not how much we have, but how much we enjoy, that makes happiness.'*
>
> *-Gurudev Sri Sri Ravi Shankar*

What the path to happiness looks like

- We start comparing ourselves to other people. Although it's awesome what they're doing, it doesn't have much to do with us and what we are capable of.

- In the end, it's about the focus on self and where we are or want to be. Those negative voices in our heads have turned into optimistic affirmations.

- We believe we are good enough, and everything's going to be all right.

- We are comfortable spending time with ourselves, and this quality time is actually thankful.

- Recharging or energy is important to everyone, and we accept it because it's natural instead of feeling bad about it.

- We will be grateful. It is a regular part of life to practice appreciation. We know there's nothing we incur, and we feel grateful for what we have.

- When others are succeeding in achieving things, we are happy because we know we are on our own path, and we are going to follow a different, but a meaningful path. We fully love ourselves, but we are happy to see others succeed.

- We know amazing things are going to happen to us because we bring positive energies into the world out there and are open to multiple experiences. Good things would find their way to us if we bring good things out into the world.

HAPPINESS IS

...being different.

Many of us are suffering from a lack of sense, direction, vitality, mission, identity, and real connection, an unhappiness that most of us have come to regard as simply ordinary. Over time, becoming natural to many of these signals, and accepting a lack of sense as natural in our lives becomes easier. We believe that in everyday life, it covers us from seeing the potential for joy and wholeness. These signs will help us understand that we are unhappy from within-

- We do not feel like we are as successful as other individuals.

- We find ourselves aiming for an impossible-to-achieve perfection level.

- Often, we are concerned that we are not good enough, smart enough, slim enough, young enough, or enough to make it in the real world.

- We feel like a victim of conditions outside our control.

- Often, we feel powerless, desperate, or sad.

- We should participate more in social activities, and belong at all times, but we rarely feel like we do.

- The struggles we experience in our life make us feel down.

- We are struggling with being able to manage love and life.

- We feel nervous, depressed, or worried.

- We feel like we are not noticed.

- Judgment for people has become more frequent for us.

- We feel dissatisfied with everything.

We see common things in different ways as we progress so that we can maximize our sense of achievement with what we already have. In order to progress further, often, the soul requires space, and this can be done with some external changes in our life. Maybe, to give the soul more space to breathe, we need to walk away from our daily work a little bit. Meditating, creating a practice of breath-work, and doing spiritual practices will also allow us to reconnect with our soul right where we are, and find peace. Perhaps all that is needed is to see life in a different way than the one we are already living. Naturally, some individuals are content alone. Yet, being alone is a challenge for some.

...taking on a challenge.

Regardless of how we feel about being alone, it is a helpful investment to build a healthy relationship with ourselves. As we spend quite a little time with ourselves, we might as well learn to enjoy it. It's important to clear up these two principles before getting into the various ways to find happiness in being alone and being lonely.

We may be a person who completely accepts the concept of loneliness. We are not friendless, social, or unloving. With time alone, we are just very happy. We are actually looking forward to it. That is just being alone, not being lonely.

We may be surrounded by family and friends, but not really linked, which makes us feel very lonely and disconnected. Or maybe being lonely only leaves us sad and looking for some company. This is what loneliness feels like. There is no point in trying to worry about our near and dear ones. We are fortunate enough to live a luxurious and glamorous life, and for those who are content with themselves, they are happy. We used to be someone who was so sad because we did think of other individuals or put their happiness first. Whether it's family or friends, we have always taken them into account. Concern is absolutely good, of course! The issue wasn't because of them, but because of the one person we should always put first. Keep in mind that our values may change as our life changes. Also be prepared under various situations to change the beliefs. As we are the only one who knows what is right for us and what is not, we are our number one priority. In order to be content with ourselves, it is our subconscious that tries to stay away from what we need to do in life. It's never too late to make the changes that we need to be happy, because we are the only one who can really take care of ourselves and make the most of life doing what we love to do, no matter what happens in life. Do not let someone else tell us that there is nothing we can do or let their judgments on how we must live our life get in the way of what is important. We must always be honest with ourselves and trust who we are, what to do, and what we need to do.

7. What disturbs our Peace?

Inner harmony belongs to those who are content with who they are, what they do, and what they have. This can be explained in just one word: appreciation. Now, we are not suggesting that we are not allowed to have ambitions, but what we are saying is that how we do this is important. Buddha said that inner harmony will come only when we get rid of strong desires as it leads to frustration and anxiety. If we are happy for what we have, when working positively for what we desire, we will find inner harmony and peace.

Inner peace is closely connected to happiness. From Buddha to Mahatma Gandhi to Dalai Lama, they all have been powerful supporters of inner peace.

In Sanskrit, the words for peace is *'Shanti'*, which relates to an individual's ethics and mental peace. In some religions, peace is used for the inner dimension rather than the outer dimension. In general, peace of mind or inner peace refers to a conscious state of calm over the possible reality of stress and pain.

The term happiness is complicated and can mean different things to different people. Happiness is generally correlated with the principles of life fulfilment. Thus, the following meaning of happiness applies to people's understanding of one's life: judgements that are seen as 'happiness'.

Can we choose between inner peace and happiness?

Given that peace and happiness are similar concepts, certain questions that come in one's mind are more important than the others. The solution to this simple question is more complex than what we would expect. Does harmony lead to happiness? Or, on the other hand, does pleasure lead to peace? In other words, the cause cannot be understood clearly. To be sure, both inner harmony and pleasure are correlated with positive feelings. Thus, having positive feelings will contribute to an improvement in one's inner peace as well as satisfaction.

What disturbs our peace?

In order to attain inner peace, we would want to explore what really lies in the way, so we can remove these things and achieve a state of calm.

The need to be validated

We are not controlling what other people are saying about us. Sure, we will impact it. But even if we do anything right, it's up to them to approve us or not. Many people just do not respect us. They may not like our smile or they may not like the colour of our eyes. No matter what the explanation is, approval from others is beyond our reach and is thus a useless discussion to be wanted. If we need affirmation from other people, we are literally being their slaves because our satisfaction depends on their judgement.

Lingering in the past

Our minds can never be calm because we can't let go of the past. If we carry previous experiences with us all the time, we are burdened with luggage that increases our weight every day. The problem is that we cannot reverse history. It has already happened. Also, we can't always trust the mind when it comes to reading from the past; the stories we tell ourselves are always unfinished. Life encounters, on the other hand, also provide us useful lessons. So, art is going to lose history without missing the lesson.

Worrying about future

How will we be peaceful if our thoughts remain in the future? The trouble with the future is that it hasn't happened yet. So, by speaking about it, we are reaching an endless number of options and 'what if's'.

It's no joke that the confusion that goes hand-in-hand with finding out what the future will bring along with anxieties and pain. This doesn't mean we are not allowed to plan; it's just that repeating thoughts in the head of future over and over again is harmful and dangerous.

Fear of death

Why are we so concerned with stopping the ageing process? There is sufficient proof that ageing is unavoidable. Or, of course, we should stretch our life by some healthier behaviour and by taking proper care of the body, but that doesn't save the body from ageing in the long run. The same is true of death: there has never been an immortal human being, and we do not see it happening in the near future.

Simply put, we are all falling and everybody's going to have to go one day or the other. How about accepting this and stop fighting the ever-changing essence of the universe? Doing that will save up not only our time but also our energy, and will help us face any stress associated with it.

Fear of unknown

Much of the people we meet have a certain uneasiness of what is unfamiliar to them. It may be the fear of travelling because they've never travelled before or the fear of people in a foreign country when they're not aware of them. We think it's normal to be extra alert when visiting new places because we never know what we are going to receive. In other words, it's a strategy in an environment that's out of balance, totally. The thing is, we just do not know about it. However, there seems to be one particular way that can help us get over all of this; it is something very simple yet significant: trust in ourselves and our loved ones.

Need to defend ourselves

In certain times, we have to protect ourselves in order to survive. But most of the time, it's just the ego that protects itself when there's no real challenge. Again, we are not influencing the world around us and what other people think. So, it's always useless to protect ourselves when someone acts in a way that we do not like. People who speak badly about other people all the time, well, that's their problem, right? It's none of our business, too. So, why are we going to waste time and energy protecting ourselves against these people? This just shows them that their comments are blessed, and that they can cheer the fact that their attacks are impacting us. The cure is simple: we have to pick our own battles.

Hatred

People who have determined for themselves that they do not like or dislike certain things, people, or circumstances, would generally either avoid or fight their strong negative feelings. When we hate something or somebody, we knowingly or unknowingly consume more energy in their way. One of the funny things is that sometimes, hatred consumes our mind so much that it blinds us to anything else. It becomes more powerful than love, family, and even friends.

So, when we do that, we are going to get hurt. Now, there's nothing wrong with things that we know are bad for us. But there is a difference between doing so in a nice and friendly manner, and doing so from a point of disrespect.

How do we rise above it?

Here's one way to promote inner peace.

Always be present in the moment. This takes a lot of practice, particularly when we are doing tasks like driving, washing, or doing our own work.

When we concentrate 100% on the job we are doing, there's no room in our head to think about things that could happen, may not happen, or did not happen. Have we heard the vocabulary in the last sentence? It could happen, could not happen, did not happen, would have occurred, or would not have happened. What do we notice about the list?

All of them are going on in our head, and the ones that happened are repeated again in our head. If we do not care about them, they're not going to happen again. We are very imaginative and can think of all kinds of disasters, but is this the right use of our mind and time? We hope we'd all agree it wasn't. How are we going to protect that from happening then?

HAPPINESS IS...

...leaving all your regrets behind.

Follow this process:

We have to be mindful of our feelings

The best way to do this is to make ourselves mindful of our emotions. If we feel nervous, stressed, frustrated or any of these negative emotions, then we are more than likely to be focusing on one of these places (may happen, may not happen, did not happen, would have happened, would not have happened). As soon as we become aware of this, switch to phase two.

We have to focus on our breathing

As soon as we know what we are doing, concentrate on our breathing. Concentrate on our pulse, then on our outer breath, and then on the few seconds of space between our inhales and exhales. This will immediately interrupt our consciousness and move our awareness into our body. We will feel fine straight away.

Finally, we have to bring our mind back on track

Once we've held our mind still and put our attention back to our body, we become completely conscious of the job we are doing presently. Concentrate on any action and detail for as long as we can.

Can we wilfully achieve inner peace and happiness?

Several ancient saints and scriptures have referred to human contact with nature for growing one's inner harmony. There are two forms of human-nature relationships that can lead to a rise in one's inner harmony and satisfaction levels.

- Short-term: take short walks outdoors on a regular basis while avoiding the use of one's mobile devices.

- Long-term: a few days of nature retreats. These retreats give us a chance to escape day-to-day pressures such as job change, work stress and so on, and to concentrate on our bodies and minds. Retreats come in different ways and sizes such as attending national parks, religious and non-religious retreat centres, among others.

To be thankful for all that we have in our life is one way to find inner peace and happiness. It has been noted that pleasure and appreciation are one and the same. For example, thankful people are more likely to notice hope and positivity in life, and this affects their understanding of life events. It has been observed that thankful people are well aware of challenges in life, but prefer not to affect by them. Instead, they highlight the interconnectivity of life, and are less driven to materialistic goals than the overall population.

HAPPINESS IS...

...a great conversation.

Having learned how to make ourselves happier, we may well be motivated to help others be happier. Is someone we love - a good friend, a partner, a relative, a son, a daughter, or another family member - unhappy? They could be going through a tough time - they could be angry and sad for whatever reason. They may be in an unhealthy relationship; they may hate their work or where they live, they could be sick, could have lost their job, or be in financial trouble. In these cases, we should be compassionate and help them achieve their own happiness. If we seek peace for other people, then we will ourselves find the direction to our inner peace.

8. Simple Ways that Lead to a Happy Life

'If we follow fun, misery follows us. If we follow knowledge, happiness follows us.'

- Gurudev Sri Sri Ravi Shankar

Happiness is one of life's most important priorities, but it seems to be meaningless for many. It's easy to say, 'Once I have that house or that car, I can finally be happy'. But, in fact, we all have happiness right now. A big house or new car doesn't make us happier; it's the beauty of living, the joy of life.

We have our moments of confidence and times of joy and bliss, but we also have to go through constant depressing emotions. There is no denying that sometimes, it becomes really difficult to find happiness, but that is what we have to focus on: it might be difficult but it will ever be impossible.

There will be bad times, of course. We have to ask ourselves, 'What comes next? How bad can it get?' We have to accept whatever the world throws at us. The sooner we accept the bad, the sooner the good will come to us. We will never know if there isn't a little darkness. Similarly, in order to achieve happiness, we need to welcome all the problems we face every day.

Life can be very easily understood in the context of a circle. If there is sadness, there will be happiness next. Therefore, if we are going through a rough time currently, we must not worry too much since it is nothing but a preparation for our happiness.

However, there are certain steps that can help us prepare our minds for the happiness:

Review the context of life

> *'See your life from the context of space and time, and you will see how tiny your life is. This connected-ness with the entire universe brings you enormous strength.'*

The Big Bang had happened approximately billions of years ago. After that, our universe has gone through a lot of phases before finally being what it is today.

If we review our life in the context of time, it will teach us the importance of time. It takes time for anything good to arrive. There are no shortcuts and there will never be any either. The short route will always be more inviting, and it might promise us a faster result, but that will only last for short period.

Patience is a good quality, and we all have to keep ourselves educated at most times to make sure that we do not fall. We are quite small compared to the universe. We are just a part of what this vastness holds for us. We are not bigger than this in any way, and must not think that way about ourselves. There is no point living in pain for the rest of our lives.

Seeing the uncertainty in life

Moments pass by, days change into weeks, then months, and then finally years. We and the life we live are in the state of constant change. Nothing lasts forever. When faced with bad luck or when negative feelings become overwhelming, it is helpful to remind ourselves of this. Almost all of us will feel sadness as a result of the loss of a loved one at some point in our lives. Many of us would feel depressed, hurt, and sad as a result of work or family issues. And some of us would be the unfortunate victims of criminal acts or wrongdoings. It is not necessary to be negative or depressed when considering these possibilities.

Be enthusiastic

There's no doubt that we will all face danger to our health over which we have no control. We can face these situations with understanding that nothing is permanent. Good things like bad ones do not last forever. It is important to recognise this in order to create a balanced viewpoint. Being mindful of the uncertainty of all situations will fill our desire to enjoy the good things in life.

Smile more

The harmful cycles of thought that many people suffer from can be solved by living in a balanced mental state based on uncertainty. Everyone wants to live with a peaceful and relaxed mind. Positive external factors certainly contribute to overall happiness, but internal factors are required to live a truly joyful life. True happiness can be experienced by mindfulness meditation and other practises such as appreciation and concentrating on the positive. People are often unhappy during tough times because they have lost some of their external attachments. Even the possibility of losing an external can bring about negative emotions in some people. When one realises that life is not eternal, and nothing is permanent, such as a partner, a child, work, physical health, financial and social status, one is more likely to respond gracefully when anything important is taken away. Attachment is the source of pain, and many people find it difficult to understand.

...understanding the power of a smile.

We do not fully enjoy our lives as long as we recognise that negative circumstances are unavoidable, and that none of our experiences are forever. All of our lives have an expiration date, including ourselves. Since everything is not permanent, attachment to ownership surely leads to dissatisfaction and setbacks. Happiness itself includes the seed of unhappiness and pain. Suffering is caused by a failure to accept life's experiences. A lot of us may not know this, but our smiles can actually make us feel happier.

What is the best place to find happiness?

We believe that the best way to look for happiness is by self-analysis.

> *'How one can improve the quality of life. This intention itself will open many doors for a person to feel better about himself.'*

Being judgmental is a bad habit which many individuals have. We've met lot of these people at some point in our lives and we've all been that person ourselves. It's often easy to observe someone else's work, but do we always attempt to observe ourselves?

Getting that 'alone' time

We do not really need to visit a location for self-analysis or self-introspection; it can be performed well in our comfort zone. There is no particular time to do this. For example, it may be handled correctly after waking up every morning or on a trip, or at tea time. It can be achieved anytime and whenever one wants after assuring that there is no one to disturb our attention.

Take a break

All of us deserve to take a holiday occasionally, and yet a lot of people keep their leisure days unused. If we are planning a holiday or a visit, it's important to take a break from work, routine, and the stresses of life in order to keep the stress levels in check.

We are not dropping our responsibility while we take a rest. We are taking care of ourselves, so we are going to have the stamina to do our best. Through learning how to watch the signs when we need a break, we are going to be able to plan some time away that will make us feel more refreshed and restored.

Communicate effectively

Effective contact seems like it's supposed to be natural. Yet in many scenarios everything goes off the track while chatting with someone. The other person hears to something else, and misunderstandings, anger, and confrontation arises. This can trigger problems in our home, education, and work relationships.

What stands as a barrier?

- Lack of concentration
- Inconsistent language of the body
- Negative expression of the body

How can we overcome this?

- We should fully focus on the speaker
- We must avoid interrupting or attempting to guide our conversation to our questions
- We need to express our concern in what's being said
- We can try to put aside our decision
- We must give our reviews

Life runs with commitment

To accomplish even the easiest of goals allows one to learn the value of dedication. Throughout our lives, we are reminded of our dedication, whether it applies to personal or career ambitions.

Learning how to commit is not just about making promises, but about maintaining those commitments in the face of expected and unexpected problems.

We work in a deeply competitive world and to say the truth, it's draining. Then what are we going to do? Are we going to stop?

We are wired to keep fighting.

The river requires two banks to flow in. The difference between the flood and the regular river is that the flow of water is controlled in the river while the water has no direction during the floods. Likewise, the energy in our lives needs to flow in some direction. Nowadays, most people are confused because there is no way in life. When we are content, there's a lot of life-energy in us; when it's not channelled, it's trapped. Commitment is necessary if life-energy is to travel in a direction. Life is working with dedication. If we look at all the little or big things in life, they're going with some effort. A student will be accepted to a school or college with a pledge.

It goes without saying that a family is always committed: the mother is committed to the child, the child is committed to the parents, the husband is committed to the wife, and the wife is committed to the husband. The greater the determination, the simpler things get. Smaller responsibility is hurting us because our power is a lot more. If we take on several roles and one of them goes wrong, we can concentrate on other jobs so that we are less distracted by the loss of that particular work. On the other hand, if we take up a single mission and it goes wrong, our job will be affected. At the speculative stage, if we take on greater responsibilities, resources are naturally attracted.

Whatever we are dedicated to, it gives us courage. If we are committed to our families, our family will support us, if we are committed to society, we will enjoy the support of society. Commitment is always going to offer excitement in the long run. One should make a commitment to making the planet a better place to live. We can't know it until we have a dream. Every idea comes from a dream. We have to dream the unthinkable. Obviously, dreaming involves something beyond our ability. We should consider the faculty that is the instructor of a dream. Some visions have had an effect on our everyday lives while others have not. Some of the visions we recall and others we've forgotten.

We are all born in this world to do something wonderful and unique; do not let this chance run by. We've got to allow ourselves the opportunity to dream and think high and big. We need courage and dedication to make those dreams that are valued to us come true. People who dreamed big were insulted for a long time, but they stayed powerful to achieve that. Do something imaginative about it. Not a year should go by without doing anything imaginative.

We have to nourish our emotions

We could be watching what we eat, writing to share our thoughts, and arranging activities that are beneficial for our overall health. Taking these steps for our well-being is wonderful, but we need to make sure that we incorporate fun and relaxation with others because it also reduces stress. Self-care doesn't have to feel like an extra task. Fun has a role to play in managing your wellbeing. There is no pressure at all. Choose what we are feeling is the easiest to start with. If we forget to do something and get off the track, we do not have to blame ourselves. Have we gone to the fast-food restaurant today instead of having a meal at home?

We just had four hours of sleep because we were busy doing other things? Next time, try to do better. Practising on a regular basis will lead us to have more energy to spend on our social life. Making time to get in contact with friends is going to help us get out of our mind while we are nervous. Feeling good about ourselves motivates us to eat better. At the end of the day, we alone can monitor the way we follow a balanced well-being. Start taking actions now and small steps will lead to long-term benefits.

An aware person once had a comment on the issue:

A person without emotions is like wood without any juice. We need to make ourselves interesting to inspire people to be with us. This will happen when we nurture ourselves with music, prayer, and service.

The way to expand from individual to universal consciousness is to share others' sorrows and joys. As we grow, our consciousness should also grow. When we expand in knowledge with time, then depression is not possible.

The way to overcome personal pain is to share universal pain. The way to expand personal joy is to share universal joy. Instead of thinking, 'What about me?', 'What can I gain from this world?' Think 'What can I do for the world?' Service leads to experience of the heart. It creates a sense of belongingness. Lack of services can lead a person to depression. Pain is unavoidable.

Suffering is optional. Pain is physical. Suffering is mental. If you are not sensitive to others' pain, then you are not a human being. That is why you need to serve. Service alone can bring contentment in life, but service without silence tires you. Service without spirituality will be shallow, and cannot be sustained for a long period. The deeper the silence, the more dynamic will be the outer activity. Both are essential in life.

When you bring some relief or freedom to someone through seva, good vibrations and blessings come to you. Seva brings merit; merit allows you to go deep into meditation; meditation brings back your smile. When you sing and pray from your heart, your emotions are nourished and you become lively.

Always be open to learning

One of the great things about life is that we've never had to stop learning. There are often new skills to learn and to adapt. If we look at the most influential people in the world, we are going to understand that. The wealthiest man in the world spends much of his time reading. The leaders in the world do not behave like they know it all. They all agree that they have to learn on an ongoing basis. In order to live life and be happy, we must constantly look for ways to change.

Learning is hard and can be difficult. This is particularly true when we talk about taking on new sports. But even if the mission is difficult, nothing is greater than our achievements. When we play sports, breaking our personal records gives us happiness like no other. The more positive the goals we set, the happier we are. And when we settle on our own goals, our happiness does not depend on others. We choose how many hours we are practising, and we take ownership of what we are doing.

When we are trying to learn as much as we can, there's less risk that we are going to come out of self-opinion. True change makers do not make themselves appear smart, they make others look smart. And when people see that we are trying to learn from them, it makes it much easier for us to like them. Every communication we have here is a chance to learn more. By keeping our minds open, we find how people present their conversations that we can learn from. It just tells us that no matter who we meet, there is still something important to learn from the experience.

Why should we be grateful for everything around us?

> 'When you practice gratefulness, there is a sense of respect toward others.'
>
> —Dalai Lama

One of the reasons why gratitude will change our lives is that it changes our attention. Life, as we already know, is all about concentration. Whatever we are focusing on, we are moving towards it. We see more of this as we exist in a state of negativity. It's easy to see things in negatives when we are we are focused on it. It's easy to see all the issues and problems when our thinking is usually directed towards it. It is also simple, in turn, to see things in positives, even when difficulties are there. When we meet a positive person, we will appreciate the reality behind any debate. And when something goes wrong, we are searching for a short cut. If they can't find one, they just claim that something positive will finally come out of everything we are going through. But it's not just about being a good person; being grateful will change our life, and it breathes positivity into everything we do. It's a change in vision, a new way of seeing life, one that requires an appreciation of the beauty of all things. We move from living in a state of scarcity to living in a state of abundance in every way we can. Even then, this isn't going to happen immediately. This change of focus takes time and the normal behaviour changes the minds.

We can quickly switch from a negative state to a positive state by counting and writing down all the things we need to be thankful for on a regular basis. The secret to this is to write it down. Writing it makes it more affirming than abstract thoughts existing in our heads.

Gratitude will change our lives by many of our worries, but at the same time, it's hard to be thankful. Fear is what happens when we are left to focus on issues that we believe are beyond our control. We are misusing the possibilities, and we are looking at our potential condition and unavoidable destruction while living in a state of panic. Yet, pain can be resolved by being thankful. When we are completely grateful for everything we have, including our issues, pain has no room to reside in our minds.

When our fear places us in a state of shortage, such as not having enough resources to pay our bills or put food in our refrigerator, we live in a state of lack rather than a state of abundance. However, being grateful put us in a state of abundance. It inspires us that we are grateful for what we have right now, at this very moment, rather than thinking about what we do not have or won't have at some future point in time.

9. Can we be truly Happy all the Time?

The human mind is a complex web of many emotions that at times are not understood. Many times, we talk about how we have a hard time trying to understand and process how we feel. It is often because we are not in touch with our inner core. There are two parts of an individual. The outer part, our body which keeps us alive, and is visible to others, and the soul, which is our inner true self remains hidden throughout, and if one is able to reach out to it, our lives change. The way we see ourselves changes in a way we could never understand. Now, when we speak of the self, we must mention how important it is to reach it. There is no known way of reaching the inner core or self. It is a journey that we have to experience by ourselves. The first part of it starts with trying to understand ourselves. It is not possible to do so, in a day. But we must not stop trying, and just like that, bit by bit, we will become more aware of ourselves-the way we are, how we feel, and things that happen around us. Out of all of emotions, happiness is one that is wanted for quite often. It overrules a lot of other emotions in a lot of cases. There might be times when these emotions get the better of us. They may destroy us at different points in our life. This would mean taking charge of our own life, and not letting our emotions overpower us. When we speak of happiness, there are certain things that come to mind. Each individual desires to have it, but why is it that only a few actually do? The entire concept of happiness is beyond our imagination or understanding. The root of the self is very different from how we see it. Looking at and understanding our habits, emotions, and ways of expression will just be equal to scratching the surface of the vastness that lies below. There are a lot of things that we will discover about ourselves as we go ahead on this life's journey. We will be surprised to see that we actually are quite different from how we thought we were. Our understanding of ourselves is bound to change every few years. There will be many phases in our life that will teach us something. But it is on us to take the learning and make something out of it. Do not ignore the signs for they are often the true calling of our self. Our 'self' is much bigger than how we carry and express ourselves. The next step is to take control of how we feel and learn to regulate it. It might sound a lot to take in at once, and it doesn't have to be that way. We must remain patient throughout. Although, being patient does not mean that we have to hold back; never do that.

It will slow down the process, leaving us more confused. Happiness does not come easily. But when it does, we often fail to notice it. We often take it for granted, and do not cherish the time until it's gone. Happiness, to say the least, is fragile. We will see that we do not observe how we feel most of the time. Keeping a check on these changes is important for us. Try to look within for the answers, always. It is the only way we can try to reach our inner self. Being in touch with it would mean being in control, remaining calm, and trying to process every emotion. Happiness can leave any time. It is going to be quick, do not be surprised when it is. Be prepared and do not worry when things go wrong. We may not be able to make happiness stay any longer, but we can certainly learn to cope with its loss. Have we been feeling good? We feel like it is going to stay that way for quite some time. We have no clue what kind of people's power hold over us. It might be a bad phone call, and we will be back to how we were feeling before, or even worse. It can spoil our entire day. That is the kind of people's power hold over us; they can entirely modify our mood. We can go from happy to hurt in minutes. Try to reach the root of such emotions. Do not let it conquer us. Get a hold of ourselves when we are feeling low, especially because of another person. Do not let them impose anything upon us. Taking our happiness away is not possible until we let it. We must let our happiness flow freely without any disturbances. We have grown up with a certain belief system and it is difficult to see life and happiness in a different way. This belief system usually arises from dependency. It reaches us in a way that we often do not notice. Dependency is the important point in all of this. We as humans are extremely dependent on external factors to find our way through to happiness. But the question is, how successful can we be? We know a lot of individuals must think that giving somebody else, the key to our happiness is a good idea, but it does not end well in most cases.

Our friendships, family, relationships; these are what surround us, keep us grounded, and make us feel loved and wanted. However, remember that no amount of love can turn into happiness unless we work towards it. Stop being under the influence that the people around us can make us feel our best, and give us all the happiness in the world. If they are, then know that it cannot last forever. One day, happiness would run out, if it depends on another individual. Do we know when it won't? When it depends only on us. We are the only people in the entire world that can make ourselves happy and sustain happiness for a long time. There will obviously be a time when we feel that we are losing our grip on it that it is slipping right out from our hands. Do not be scared for it is natural for something like this to happen. Material things make everyone happy or so they think. But there is a huge difference between thinking that we are happy, and actually achieving peace and happiness in our lives. We must not associate our happiness with material things as it would only bring us temporary happiness. Do not run after something which is temporary and which will go away. This is a way to postpone the happiness we feel. Attaching the entire value of our happiness to material things would mean that it depends on them, and that is not a good practice at all. However, this idea of happiness does not seem to go away that easily. Once an idea is stuck, it is difficult to get rid of it. Ideas often do that to us, lead us off the path, and make us believe and do things that might not be true to who we are as individuals. If we were to note an example, there will be multiple examples. What do people mostly associate happiness with? Wealth, health, success, and education- these are the most common things people look for to make themselves happy. But, as we all can see, there are many of individuals out there who have all these but are still unhappy;

unhappy with their lives, their emotional state, and other things. There can be hundreds of reasons why an individual may feel that way, and it is not on us to understand every bit of it. But what we can understand and control is how we deal with our situations, and what we believe in. It starts from doing away with the idea of happiness being associated with wealth. Everybody asks, though in different ways, how can we be happy? How do we check the negative? How can our life dream be carried out in the way we want it to be?

We offer this question almost as if sad incidents are not pleasant and need not only be minimized but absolutely removed. As I flip through Facebook posts during the morning, posts from gurujis, quotes from Holy Scriptures, mythological tweets, and life experiences from friends, we ask these questions to ourselves. Our minds get affected by all these too soon in the morning, and we become unable to handle ourselves. We would really like to have a clear formula that helps us sort out the quotations, lectures, pictures, and video clips in a way that we can quickly understand and apply when feel disturb.

At these moments, the lovely quotations, stories are difficult to remember. There are many philosophical practices And They concentrate on facts, life and what is real around us. Surely, then, some shinning soul must have thought of an answer to our fundamental question in the old days: How can we be happy? They did actually, and provided a model that could be converted into method of action in turn.

Recognize the example in our lives and we can bring all the quotes and stories into practice quickly, and because it is not directly related to any one religion, it is universal. The model emphasis is spiritual, so it's not about near to God as much as near to oneself. In our hands is our happiness.

HAPPINESS IS

...yoga.

The essence of ancient philosophy lies in the Upanishads. Although Vedic hymns are incantations to gods or sacrifice laws, the Upanishads deal with the supreme conscience and make no mention of any deity. It is our fact that we exist in a world of alive and not alive objects, and must therefore be directed by dharma in order to fulfil our desires. As always, it's about balance and not one being more important than the other in philosophy, Ayurveda or food. The distance between learning and doing still remains. Knowing the model just doesn't mean that we are satisfied.

The second model is about practising it. Shift only occurs when we have *gnana* or knowledge of the model, *bhakti or* feeling it and believing it in our hearts and *karma* or showing it in motion. There are three types yoga; it is not just body movement but also healthy diet and balanced thinking. Deep in our souls, we need to feel. Reading the poetry of the saints of *bhakti* and absorbing the flavour by meditating and taking the images of the relationships we most admire to our inner eye. So, in our hearts, there is great kindness, and we are close to our ideal. It's *bhakti*. Finally, there is *karma*, which ultimately transforms the knowledge of the mind and heart into action. Let's work on an example: if we do not predict future events or if events do not occur according to our schedule, we appear to be worried about the future. Fear also causes us to do things that hurt our relationships at home and work because of our anxiety. So, in our acts, we are not 'Dharmik'. This is now applied to our present state of being and runs through each box. It's *gnana*. And, by looking at what parts of our body are affected, we manifest this into our hearts and bodies. If we are tensed about the money, our heads, ears, minds, and stomachs will be affected by the overall tension. We are committed to another action: listing what our long-term financial targets are, so we have a clearer understanding of what we need.

We look for things in the garden that soothe us, or start our morning with music and body asanas to remind us to enjoy life. We enjoy eating food in peace rather than having it in a rush. With our every action or feeling, we consider whether relationships are regular and genuinely improving. Of course, this all sounds very okay, but bhakti and karma are not easy and need practice. They also need reminders and discipline regularly, and that's where rituals and *puja* come in. *Puja* is a way for us to hit the pause button and ask ourselves if we are working towards bliss by focusing our thoughts on our mind, heart and body. Unfortunately, instead of being a chance to look inward, *puja* has now weakened to dealing outside with the Gods rather than heading inside to realize how one need not be satisfied all the time, and that life's ups and downs are unavoidable. This is simple, but it will slowly become practice if we have a daily checking method such as *puja* or meditation practices, and regularly ask ourselves if we are practicing Dharma and surrounding ourselves with like-minded people. We can always need a reminder, but we can understand that we can extract every little of happiness from any situation in life by reminding ourselves that we can't always be perfect. Our lives feel difficult most of the time, but these are a few habits or ways that can take us closer to being truly happy.

1. Yoga helps a lot. It is an ancient Vedic path that offers many methods to help bring back our external consciousness and understanding while also moving inward within ourselves. The term 'Yoga' is far broader than just keeping a balanced body. Starting with yoga asanas (postures) is a great beginning to go on

to the deeper secrets of human consciousness's union with that of the cosmos. Think about why we want to do yoga in the first place before attending any yoga class: is it simply for body, do we want a more thoughtful, deep approach, or do we just want to see what it's all about? Keep an open mind and as we practice, be mindful of what's going on inside ourselves. There are several yoga variations, some are straight forward, some are powerful, and some are mindful. If it doesn't work out in our first one or two lessons, do not give up.

2. Ayurveda is an ancient holistic science that takes the air we breathe, the food we consume, the energy we are made up of, and the environments we live in into account. How the world around us is explained depends on how aligned we are with our bodies and minds. Start by taking an honest look at ourselves, the food we consume, and the way we live. The first step is merely being aware. Get an evaluation of our form of energy that will give us strong reasons for Ayurvedic ideas that are right for us.

3. We can do meditation as well; as it soothes our nerves and makes us feel better from the inside. It's important to have a time and place set aside, so we have it built into our day. Start with 10 minutes. This leads to making it a habit. Do not seek outcomes. When we've just begun meditating for a few days, it's hard to measure results. There is a slow and

continuous process for meditation to achieve long-term benefits, so stick with practice. There are many meditation variations, and all of them work. A variation that works for us, we have to find.

4. The energy of life itself is Prana. It is all the energy in the entire universe, sometimes deep, sometimes solid. It makes flowers bloom, babies smile, people breathe, and they make the world go round. Pranayama is the art of aligning ourselves through our breathing with this force. We will find that it is a powerful way to focus on energy when we begin paying attention to our breathing. Look for a class in Yoga that also provides pranayama. It is not advisable to perform pranayama without guidance. Start out slow and thin. No hurry to do something. Pay full attention to what is going on inside us as we are practising pranayama. The results are otherwise wasted.

5. Words carry great power. Enter the company of those whose positive words and thoughts are for us. Try to let go of friends or people who do not provide us with positive energy.

6. If we have no skill to which we belong, establish one. Start having debates on we want to have. It might be a book club, a forum online, or a weekly session of meditation. Think about whom we look up to, who we think we are referring about, or who we'd like to be as we grow up whenever we can. There's

a saying: 'The teacher arrives when the student is ready'. We must be open to the people who turn up in our lives.

7. As retreats in modern times have become popular, finding one that fits our needs. Starting with one that provides direction along with plenty of time alone. Prepare to unplug completely from your phones and computers ahead of time.

8. We know that adequate sleep is an important source of good health, brain activity, and emotional well-being, no matter how many modern times directs us towards less sleep.

9. Every night, most adults require about 7 or 8 hours of sleep. Our body may tell us that it needs more rest if we find ourselves fighting the urge to nap during the day or just generally feel like we are in a cloud. We should have a clearer understanding of how we are doing after a week. Go to bed and wake up every day, weekends included, at the same time.

   - Set aside the hour before bed as a silent time. Take a bath, read, or do enjoyable activities.

   - Keep it dark, calm, and quiet in the bedroom.

   - Try restricting it to 20 minutes if we have to take a nap.

HAPPINESS IS...

...meditating.

These are how we can get closer to being happy, but there is no such way that can lead us to truly being happy all the time. Life is a rocky road and we must take it as it comes. Be fearless, and happiness will follow.

10. Looking Within for Happiness

What *is* happiness?

The definition does not remove its meaning entirely. Happiness refers to a class of terms relevant to all particular cases, which can be even more clearly understood by the examples of family members. We speak a lot about the joy of relationship, but it isn't always easy to achieve. Therefore, the Vedas also have a lot of knowledge about contentment. This is a kind of happiness for those who have not yet completely formed a sense of love. Any method of growth has its own stages. Happiness is achievable if we practice selflessness and act without thinking about own benefits and be generous, loving and giving to people attitude. At the start of the spiritual journey, the new feelings and emotions that emerge on this path can hardly be understood by a person. The whole thing is not clear and looks doubtful. Impressions of materials still remain fresh and solid. They are inviting us to adopt an old idea. When we feel new kinds of joy which were silent before, now new emotions often emerge. This is the pleasure of spiritual purification, self-realization, and spiritual association. At the same time, it makes us happy and sometimes scares us.

People say that one should feel pleased with following: one's family members, food, and money that they have. Let's start with the first point: being happy with your family. The desire to please the family is the basic component of preparation for spiritual satisfaction.

How do we identify the members of a family? These are the ones we have to associate with because even though we want to reject them, go to another country or try to forget them, we can't completely cut off ties with them. Therefore, relationships with family prepare us for the fact that we will still have eternal relatives in our spiritual life. So, on the basis of knowing eternity at once, we must learn to communicate. All in all, the true reality is our senior relatives. And if even with ordinary people we can't sustain relationships, how are we going to practice yoga and build relationships with our relatives.

Yes, relationships in the material world only apply to one's life. But it would be very sufficient if we spend it learning to connect, so as not to detach from our relationships. Spiritual happiness includes our understanding of relationships that are permanent in nature. We will never be able to approach the higher levels of happiness if we do not enjoy this relationship in our heart. The more we know that we are linked with each other eternally, the happier we become. If one has realized that family life must be guided so that relationships never break during this life, one has progressed for the higher stage of love that goes beyond the reach of one life. It implies that one is ready for the spiritual world.

Ultimately, we need to say a few things about being happy with an honest life. One should be pleased with the amount of wealth obtained by honest effort. As a result of cheating, happiness won't come. Therefore, we should find such a work that we can be sure that without being involved in any wrong doing, we are getting honest results for honest work.

It is argued that a human's well-being requires a larger range of factors than just satisfaction. This involves personal development, intention, control of one's own world, and self-directedness, as well as enjoyment and lack of pain. The assumption is that pleasure is a wrongly limited aim to be achieved at the expense of attractiveness or meaning. Actually, since things like beauty and intention are very complicated and demanding, we should not usually take short-term satisfaction to follow them.

Happiness is typically spoken of as a healthy position, and this is important for the level of enjoyment. There are some important variations between negative and positive feelings. Every positive emotion is the same, but every negative emotion is negative in its own way. That is, each negative emotion comes with a clear picture about what kind of thing is going on and what a solution would be.

If one begins to think that he has learned everything and feeling complete, avoids learning spiritual teachings, which means two things.

Either the absolute reality was not what he was learning, or he was setting selfish material expectations for himself. A happy person never believes in a nutshell that he has learned anything. He is gradually convinced that he knows little, and thus makes every attempt to at least understand something.

The same view on meditation and every other form of spiritual self-improvement is taken by a happy man. Spiritual life is about the real reality getting closer. We've only just started. Dissatisfaction with level of self-realization is thus the sign of inspiration and determination to travel this journey until the end.

Why is contentment, for us, so important? We are good with everything when we are happy. Only one condition is possible: we really have to realize that we deserve a lot more than what we have. We most possibly benefit from the most extreme punishment. So, we should understand that any time we run into trouble, judging by things we have done in this world, we must have brought the world of trouble upon ourselves. And thus, negativity is reduced somewhat. They are moving much more smoothly than one would expect. We must, therefore, be thankful, forever grateful. In other words, satisfaction is knowledge of the total truth's grace and appreciation.

A brief view of happiness

Though it may appear like today everybody is in search of happiness, it is not as easy to achieve it. In order to be content, we need to have a few things in our lives to look for—things that mean something and make sense to us, that interest us, that we want to be interested in, and to make us feel positive. As social people, we need to communicate with others; to link and know as we belong to others.

The man told the child that loving himself is the first precondition for being happy. The reality of self-love is to feel happiness. We have to offer our life worth in order to achieve this. Take care of our physical well-being and health. It's also important to realize that in this universe, we are special beings. That implies that each of our goodness and faults are the product of the universe's history. We are no better or less than anyone else, just the effects of millions of particular causes. Thinking about being the best or getting a better life, but just leaving it as a thought, is one of the things that can make people unhappy. This only adds to anger and regret. If we think something should or should be done by us, simply do it. We do not have too much to pause about.

It is also important for our behaviour to be aligned with your words. If we think in one way, but behave in another, we are only going to generate uncertainty. Instead, everything flows more naturally when there is peace in the inner universe.

'Take control of own actions instead of worrying about whether others are going to make it or not. 'We will suffer if we allow hatred to bloom inside our hearts. And it will be harmful to our pain. If we continue to feel good about others' achievements, our happiness will be multiplied. In order to achieve anything, we will have to have more power inside our hearts.

Harmful assumptions we make of ourselves

We have learned a great deal of happiness till now. Now, we will focus on the things that stand as a limit to happiness. For, it is only when we will be entirely aware that are disrupting our self, can we remove them once and for all. There can be times when we will be able to clearly see that happiness is within our control, we might have expectations to believe that happiness is not possible for us.

'We are undeserving of happiness'

We can find like we do not deserve happiness; we do not deserve to be happy because of what we've done wrong in the past. We have taken the wrong option to do anything or not to do anything. We blame ourselves; we feel a sense of disappointment and guilt, and we wish we could reverse the decision we made. Maybe we are sorry for something we did or didn't do. We could have done something to hurt or hurt someone else, and now we feel guilty; we feel shame. We think it would be unfair to try to be happy. If that's the case, we need to know that sorrow and shame really has a good intention.

Happy people learn to move on with their mistakes. We should do the same thing. Avoid what we did wrong. Agree that what has been done is done and cannot be changed. There's nothing we can do with that. Although, we should change the next thing we do.

It might be, however, that we didn't do anything wrong. Yet, we know it. We can feel bad that we can't ease someone's pain. If that's the case, we are still going to feel the guilt. This occurs when we feel bad about incidents that, in truth, we are or are not responsible for. We can feel, for example, that we can't afford to be happy when other people in our life are unhappy: our sibling has been unable to look for work or our partner is under stress; our sister is unable to get a good college, or a good friend's dad has expired. Yet, feeling unworthy doesn't help anyone. We've done nothing wrong by being happy and showing that we are happy. If we are worried about other's problems, realize that finding happiness is the best thing to do, and then we are in a stronger place to support others to be happier.

'We do not deserve forgiveness if we cannot forgive'

It's not because we believe that we've done anything bad, it's because somebody else has done us wrong. We may have been cheated on by a friend, or we have suffered injury as a result of someone else's acts. We do not accept that we should be happy, and we just can't forget. Yet, forgiveness does not mean giving up, weaken, excusing, or ignoring the offence; the other person is also responsible for their acts.

Other person does not bound to be forgiven for our unhappiness, sorrow, and pain, but we deserve to be free from this negativity. Forgiveness is for us, not for the other person. Forgiveness involves letting go of the guilt, anger, or irritation we have as a result of someone else's actions. It means no longer wanting revenge. Accept and agree that what has been done is done and cannot be changed. But the only thing that can change is what we do next.

'Accept people and situations as they are in life and then take action. The moment you do this, you will see you are out of the confusion about anything in life.'

Even though we do not have the will to forgive right now, we can always learn to manage the wrongdoing of the other person as we strive for happiness.

'We can never get back the happiness we once lost'

Maybe, though, it's not our own or anyone else's faults in the past that stops us from finding satisfaction. Do we look back to other times and situations of our life and believe like everything was so much better than that? Have we been happier? There's nothing wrong with thinking about the past- looking back at happier moments in our life – but living on those times will hold us trapped into believing that we are never going to be that happy again.

We've got to put things in understanding. It's easy to admire the past, to decline, overlook, or ignoring the problems that might have happened during the happy days. Even if we go back to how we were when we were younger, it wouldn't be the same thing. If the experience was too pleasant, or if we admire it, focusing on the past keeps us away from the opportunities at the moment. As someone once said, 'We can't launch the very next chapter of the book if we keep on reading the last one again.'

'We cannot be as happy as them'

It may be because we feel that happiness is for other people. We associate ourselves with them, see that they are happy, and conclude that our life will never be the same as theirs. That's right, we can't. Our lives would not be the same at every point. We are too special to compare ourselves with others; our talents, abilities, contributions, and importance are unique to us and to this world. They should never be compared to anyone else. There's still someone that we meet, learn about, or read about in books, magazines, and social media to associate ourselves with. There's still someone we can see doing more than us and thus being happier than us.

But comparing our worth, our talents, our chances, our advancement, our growth, etc. to others will only make us feel inferior. If we are going to be satisfied, we need to let go by stopping comparing ourselves to others. Jealousy is incompatible with pleasure, so if we continually compare ourselves to others, it's time to quit. Instead, be motivated by others, and with the help of this book, start preparing how we can move forward. This would make us feel positive and in charge, so we are no longer looking for what the other person has that we do not have – we are going to be busier moving on to what we want.

HAPPINESS IS...

...self-confidence.

'We cannot be happy until something big happens'

Are we waiting for anything to happen before we can be happy about it? Can we think that we are only going to be satisfied when a perfect friend or when a perfect career or a new home comes along? We may be waiting for a friendship to end, a neighbour to pass, or someone to die, or we might assume that we can only be satisfied until we are healthier, lose weight, or get more fit.

It's tempting to believe that happiness is all that we can find until all the stars are aligned and something else is truly in order in our life. Yet, this is just a story that we've been telling ourselves. Happiness is not incidental. And that's good news, actually; we do not have to wait to be happy. Instead, we should learn to be happy when we are waiting for the right friend, the perfect career, or whatever we are wishing for. When it comes to happiness, a journey is as important as a destination; a journey is part of happiness.

11. How can we achieve happiness through people?

'Events bring you small joy, while existence brings you happiness and bliss.'

-   Robin Sharma

We have discussed all the reasons we cannot achieve happiness. It mainly focussed on ourselves. Now, we will focus on the different ways in which we can get a step closer to happiness through others.

It often happens that we identify our goals and realise what we really want when we help others, or make efforts to support them in a difficult situation.

The way success connects to our happiness is one of the ways of loving other people. When someone we care about is sad, it is not shocking that we feel it too. Emotions spread, and happier people have a positive effect on their friends and family's lives. It's also the cause for depressed people having a negative effect on the people who surround them.

It is not only worrying and disappointing if someone we like is frustrated, but it is irritating from a personal point of view; it does not make us comfortable, and we do not want to feel that way.

Since we do not wish to feel like this, we just try and attempt to make them feel better.

This is not crazy, but the greater our importance is on the disappointment of someone else, the more our success is dependent upon them. We must separate our thoughts from theirs. We must see our bad luck with them as separate from their pain. We will not do our job, aim, or initiative to 'improve' them and make them happier if we want another person to be happy, or if we really believe that we have the best responses for them. This does not mean we disregard them, but we need to help them find their own comfort and ideas rather than taking credit for someone's happiness. But how do we make a difference by helping the dissatisfied person?

That might help us with that:

We must give them the time to process

There is always a solid reason behind the unhappiness of people: a loss, a painful feeling, or something even more extreme. After a while, most people go back to their basic level of satisfaction. We must be patient. We really have no better way to do it than to accept what they feel and let them know that if they need us, we are there to listen.

We must always be understanding

We must rely upon our idea of an event or circumstance, and our emotions so that we can contribute to the feelings that someone else might feel. But note that in a particular situation, they may feel or believe otherwise. The bottom line about understanding is that we can't get it. We do not have to live the same thing that they did, we do not have to accept that we'd feel the same way; we only have to understand the sentiment and feelings of the other person, and know more or less that they're having a tough time.

...being nice.

Talking is not always the answer

It is not reasonable to assume that they need us to deal with their unhappy feelings all the time. If people are sad, it is not easy to be around them, so we give them space and give ourselves space too. It is important to recognize that what we can do to help someone else is always minimal. Acceptance of what is achievable and knowledge of our limits will make us feel less powerless. We have to be our natural and cheerful self. It's not all right to be grateful because someone we love is sad. The more secure and positive we are, the more we are willing to help and inspire others.

How we can make them happy?

We can help them identify their goals

For all of us, this is the same. In our lives, all of us need reason and meaning. We need to try for something; we need to reach destination. We need to discuss what we want and what we want to focus on with the other person. Perhaps, they would like to change and learn new skills.

Encourage the other person to take those steps in order to move forward. Enable them to work out and step by step what they should do.

Encouragement is key

The one thing that they want is for us to support them by motivating them. They might have to be encouraged to pause – to stop doing anything – but they may also have to be encouraged to start something even during the difficulties. We can think of a moment when someone else has inspired us. Maybe, someone just took an interest in what we did and what we wanted. Has their support changed positively? We must act in the same way.

We might inspire someone to take a step, continue, do challenging work, or do something they did not feel confident enough to do before. Find out what our issues are if we are weakening. It doesn't mean that we disregard the difficulties to inspire others. Rather, consider the difficulties and reassure them that they can resolve the issues. Identify the abilities and resources that allow them to achieve. Remind ourselves of our motivation for doing this; remind what we will achieve, and remind how we will better ourselves or our situation.

But do not wait until something good has been achieved. Say something when you see someone progressing; praise them. Identify their inputs and highlight their achievements. If we are thinking of an inspiring idea, share it!

Give a compliment

In reality, complimenting someone else will raise happiness quickly; they can make their day, it can even be remembered for the rest of their lives! There are several explanations for compliments – whether they've achieved something, made a special effort, or put extra time into something for others. So, tell them! We do not have to think about changing the words. To say the truth uncomfortably is better than not saying anything at all.

First of all, we can start by thanking the other person. Be particular. The most special compliments are sometimes the most memorable because that shows that we noticed.

Find ways to congratulate people for their acts, special qualities, the care and patience of a person, or their extra time for something. Note what we wear and what it feels like. Compliment the appearance and make people feel good. Notice when somebody's working. They may be somebody who helps in a shop or café, or someone in your workplace. Please comment positively on their work or company.

Look around to see who we can congratulate today. We do not just keep it to ourselves if we like what someone has done, just do it. Tell them! Let the other person know that we have noted their efforts or acts, and help them to feel satisfied with their abilities.

...giving a gift
for no reason in particular.

We must be vocal about our appreciation

Make attempts to thank people sincerely. Explain the beneficial impact of their efforts. We feel comfortable and we feel satisfied if we know that we've made a difference. So, if we have a good impact on what someone has done, explain how.

When we suggest to another person that he has made a positive change, they will then feel well about themselves because of their effect on us, whether it's a friend listening to us, a business, or someone who has given a good service.

HAPPINESS IS...

...accepting people
for who they are.

When we respect and accept someone or something, we understand the importance of something a person has done or has given us: their commitment, their time, guidance, or encouragement. Yet, gratitude can and should always only be remembered and expressed. Thank you and gratitude are just words. But we express our feelings with action when we display gratitude for something. It doesn't have to be a great action; it just shows our gratitude.

12. Focus on What Matters

'Do not focus on what others want. See what it is that you want. When you stop looking inside and look at others that is when you miss the boat.'

- Gurudev Sri Sri Ravi Shankar

Focus is important to our happiness and lives altogether. We are all going through the everyday changes. It's what guides us to do the best we can do. However, when we try to achieve so much in so little time, it can also distract us from achieving our ultimate objectives. It reduces self-worth and our confidence in us. We cannot achieve our full potential if we are not focused. Focus is directly related to our happiness. We can consider it a tool to achieve all that we want, mostly happiness. The way our focus shifts is responsible for our feelings. This happens because focus allows us to fix our mind on one thing, which automatically makes way ways for more productivity. There are certain ways in which focus plays a huge role in our lives, so much that it may change it entirely, for the better. We are living in a fast world where a lot of things can easily distract us every day. We may do anything, but it is very difficult to succeed if we lack concentration in our life. Focus will change everything, truly. As it is said, 'where attention goes, energy flows'. It expands as we concentrate on something. It is important to know why concentration is so important, so we can use it to our advantage. Here are the reasons why concentration is important in our lives. Focus will allow us to expand our awareness and intelligence. Our awareness will gradually grow as we begin to concentrate on learning. Rely on day-to-day learning of new things. In our life, make learning a priority. There will be distractions around us but we need to concentrate anyway. When we concentrate on expanding our awareness or understanding, our lives will grow automatically. Distraction is always going to kick our doors. What we choose between attentions versus distractions, is our decision. Attention will assist us in our work to become more effective. As a primary target, it will allow us to attract our attention to a specific mission. Everything that is secondary. Focus on being productive, but the majority of individuals never focus on being productive. They focus on being busy instead. In order to become highly efficient at work and get the job done effectively, focus is important in our lives. The number of achievements we attain in life will be decided by our attention. When we place our attention on achieving something in life, we will achieve those. Otherwise, our time and energy will end up being wasted on pointless things. Life is like a camera that focuses on and records what is important. If we want to achieve our objectives, place our attention on the target and keep working until we reach them. When we are focused, no one can stop us from running. Successful individuals focus on their mission. Every single day, they focus on their targets. This helps them achieve success more easily than anybody else. Most individuals, however, attempt everything but never remain constant. It becomes their block of lane. In order to achieve the success, we desire, attention is necessary in our lives. Successful individuals never allow distractions to get in their way. It is crucial to have freedom within us, this would make sure that no matter how many people and how many problems we come across, we will always get past them. Life as we know it has both a positive and a negative form to it but that does not mean that we can stop and give up on ourselves. If one person comes to us with their issues we must not get too involved in their issues because it can distract us from our path. We must help them in every way possible without getting involved. We must keep our interests and energy perfect in order to help those in need. If we only start weakening, what can we expect from those who want our help? Truthfully, being unbothered is an art form as a whole which needs daily practice.

HAPPINESS IS...

What happens when we stop allow ourselves from being bothered by others? In our own terms, we can finally start living life. Without feeling judgement from others, we take care of what we want. When we are worried by what others think of us, it is difficult to be happy. The world around us should revolve around us. It may sound selfish, but that is the point. This is the most important move in staying unbothered.

This is how we can understand that it is important to not be disturbed:

- Giving ourselves priority means doing what's best for us. We must ask ourselves if this is what we want or if this is what someone else wants for us. If we do what someone else wants us to do, we are not going to put ourselves first. Even when it made us sad, we would always place our friends' needs above our own. We will finally feel free until we begin prioritizing ourselves. We shouldn't care about what other people want.

- The next step is to choose our friends carefully. We can think of a lot of people or individuals who have been a part of our lives but have somehow ended up discouraging us. Putting other people's happiness first can do a great deal of harm that we may not realise sooner, but the impact remains. We get into the habit of putting others before us, It makes us feel soften of love and care. We become too busy with finding solutions to other people's problems rather than ours. In this process we forget to focus on what really matters.

- Be it studies or a personal life, a person without focus won't go any far. We must always remember that we do not need to keep unnecessary people hanging around in our lives. There might be times when we feel that we can hardly focus on ourselves because we are too involved in other people's lives.

- We must ask ourselves a few questions before carrying people ahead through the course of our life. The first and most important question is how these people make us feel from inside. If our answers do not be like happiness, we should take it as the first red flag. There is no point in putting ourselves through pain because of another person who would not matter in coming years.

- The next question should be about what they bring to our life, their contribution. This is largely related to the first point of how they make us feel. We should always understand how we are when they are around us. This is important because if we are not ourselves around them, they are not the correct kind of people for us. If we are talking about friends, close ones, we must feel secure and real around them. There is no point of being false here, and if there is, know that it is not genuine.

These three questions are far more important than we realise, but we need to ask ourselves these. We will narrow down and discover who our true friends are when we ask ourselves questions about various friendships. Not all partnerships are planned for a lifetime.

The fewer mates we have, the fewer problems we are going to face. Do we prefer to have a 'hundred rusty coins or four glossy quarters?'

Of all steps in the remaining unbothered process, to get rid of toxic people has to be the toughest. We are forced to act, to look at our experiences, and see whether they work for us or against us.

It is none of our business what other people think of us. It's their opinion and it doesn't affect us. Does that make sense there? There is no easier way of saying it.

We are all so concerned with how we are viewed by other people even when we know that the feelings of other people are not our concern.

Keeping to us is another part of minding our own affairs. Do not disturb anybody with our drama, and other people will not disturb us. This makes life a lot simpler. All we need to do is start minding our own business and focus on our issues rather than other people's. If an individual has an issue with us, it is not on us to explain ourselves to them. We stop explaining and start keeping to ourselves because that is the only way out of these situations and the best thing, we can do is keep ourselves away from these kinds of people. All that they bring us is pain and self-doubt. Living is more about our will power than it is about our actions. Once we believe and are ready to let go of a toxic situation, then only can we truly feel free. We will always let our situations rule our heads. Leaving physically does not matter as much as leaving mentally does. Our mental health needs to be prioritised above all. The most important thing to remember is to not let our emotions overpower us. People's understanding of us might matter but as we walk along, we will see how little value it holds.

Our gut feelings are equally important on our path to happiness. As we talk about focus, we must not forget that our decisions make us reach where we are. If we are in a happy place mentally, there will be less need for doubt. However, if we do not feel good on a particular day, we might go back to doubting ourselves all over again. A lot of us happened to have made a few decisions that we regret and might continue doing so for the rest of our lives. What has happened earlier cannot be changed. But what can be changed is our understanding towards life and how we deal with our mistakes. Regret might sound common but it has the power to take us down to a place where there is no recovery. All that we have to do is let go of the regret and focus more on learning from the mistake. Do not hold it as it will cause us more pain. Learning is a long process with certain points to it. Not following our gut feelings can cause us a lot of trouble. We might be doubtful in the beginning but once everything starts in place, we will realise how effective it can be. Forgiving ourselves for our mistakes is important, in fact, it is the first step towards healing. Learning is a fantastic idea as it is lying right in front of us, only if we are willing enough to see. We must know what we want for ourselves. We must hold something as long as it does not make us feel stable. Following our gut feeling won't get us into trouble; it will help us understand ourselves better.

Finally, do not be scared to say no to anybody.

Maybe we are nice people at heart, and it's always been a struggle to say no.

When we do not say no, we generally do it for someone else to please. To say no is to take control of our lives and to do what we want to do. This is linked to our gut feelings. To help us with focus, we can be more careful with ourselves. When we become conscious, there are certain ways of calming ourselves down. We appear to take fast, not deep breaths when we are nervous or upset.

The next step is to accept that we feel out of breath. We should allow ourselves to say we are nervous. The anger that we experience can decrease when we mark how we feel and encourage ourselves to express it.

Having useless thoughts that do not actually make sense is part of being nervous or frustrated. Challenging thoughts might seem to be very difficult in the beginning but with a little help from the people around us, we can make it. We are capable of achieving anything that we want, and we do not have to be sorry about it. Feeling calm has a lot to do with how we deal with the situation at hand. The moment we start panic, we go far from being calm. We must show some amount of self-control if we are expecting to feel better. We must ask ourselves if what we feel has any meaning to it. Second, balanced thoughts do not make us over think, and we must be aware of this fact. Whenever we find ourselves over thinking, we should not leave our thoughts as that would be equivalent to turning our backs on ourselves. There is nothing sadder than that. We can understand if there is any sense behind our current thought process. If we are able to find a solid reason, we may go ahead and do something about it. However, if there is nothing found, we must keep ourselves away from that specific train of thought.

Taking a break from our stress to concentrate on a workout will help us relax while also growing. Physical exercise in any form can relieve stress, improve our mood, and help us to think more clearly. Meditation improves our ability to stay in the present moment and address life's challenges with greater focus, calmness, and purpose. Taking our minds off the things happening around us is not the solution. We have to face them but only in time. Giving ourselves some time is not wrong, it helps us manage better. By concentrating on the positive and reducing our negative thoughts, we will improve our happiness. Overall satisfaction is affected by positive and negative feelings. When our brain is attacked with negative thoughts, it responds by generating tension and depression in our bodies. When we think more positive things, our brain relaxes and becomes happier. After we've become aware of your negative thoughts and feelings, and worked to oppose them for a few days, they'll start to move away. We will be able to focus more on what we want to do without being distracted by negative feelings. We would be more energetic as a result of this. The best part is that it would make us happier.

- Take 30 minutes to think and write down all the positive thoughts that come to mind. Create a list of the people and places in your life that bring us joy: good friends, favourite holiday destinations, childhood memories, and so on. Create a list of things that make us happy, such as puppies, infants, the scent of old books, or a good dinner.

- Pay attention to our reflections for the whole week. When we find ourselves thinking or feeling something negative, sad, or upsetting, remember that it's completely natural. Simply pay attention and make a note of them.

- The number of negative thoughts and emotions usually decreases after a few days. When we change negative thoughts with positive ones so fast, it's almost as if the brain gets irritated with being negative. Make efforts to think positive thoughts during the day to improve. Decide to think of positive thoughts while driving car and so on, so that we can only think positive thoughts.

- Do not pass judgement on ourselves and our actions. Throughout the day, everybody has a lot of sad feelings. Do not worry if we are having negative thoughts; it's perfectly normal. As we put our happy thought to mind, force a smile on our face. This will aid in the removal of the negative thoughts. Do not go a day without challenging the negative feelings and replacing them with positive ones.

The majority of people aspire to be happy. Though each person may have their own unique understanding of what each of those things means to them, the desire to live a life free of stress, concern, and fear, while also being full of happiness and achievement, remains constant. Even though we all want to be happy and good in life, that isn't always the case. We usually spend more time involved in negative emotions than positive. We just can't seem to overcome the tension associated with daily problems, whether it's in our relationships, finances, jobs, well-being, or goals. It's no surprise that we spend so much of our time depressed. So, how do we go about reversing this trend? What are the secrets to a happy life? Is that something that can be attained in real life?

HAPPINESS IS...

...being in the moment.

However, there is a way to happiness. It's just that a lot of people do not want to drive on those highways. They're less known to navigate. Most people will turn around because the beginning is often rocky and some parts of the road are almost closed. Many willing to put in the effort, however, will ultimately find themselves on more manageable roads. However, walking along them at first may be risky. But it can be done, one step at a time, one day at a time, with the right amount of effort. Happiness is available to us if we are prepared to put in any effort. The thing about happiness and achievement is that in order to achieve, we must first have a clear understanding of what this means to us. Some say that money is the only thing that's important. But, as many people are unaware, wealth does not always bring happiness. Do we want to be content? It's no problem. It's possible that we are content right now. Happiness is attainable right now, regardless of what is going on in our life. Whether we agree with that affirmation or not, we've most certainly heard it before. Consider and write down what will make us happy. We will be one step ahead of the game until we find out what all of those words mean to us. However, we must then add energy to it. We will need to take a few steps and develop routines to help us get there. Overall, these are important keys to happiness that will assist us in realising both in our lives.

13. Finding Happiness in Other Activities

> 'It's not that some people have the willpower and some don't. It's that some people are ready to change and others are not.'
>
> -Stephen Covey

To put it simply, willpower is nothing but our willingness to change something: a situation in our life, a certain relationship with a person, or even a habit.

Willpower, as we can see, varies from one person to another. One other factor that remains attached with willpower is motivation. Before we inquire into the specifics of willpower, let us understand the elements that are related to it.

Motivation

It's what prompts us to behave, whether it's having a drink of water or reading a book to learn. In common use, the word motivation is sometimes used to explain why a person does something. It's the driving force behind our behaviour. We are all different when it comes to how we get inspired. Depending on the scenario, we could be more motivated to complete a task because it makes us feel good rather than the reward, while in other cases, it is the reward that motivates us to finish the task.

In what ways can motivation help us?

Motivation can be defined as the majority of the activities we perform at work, whether we know it or not. When we complete a job on time, it's because we do not want to get in trouble. When we respond to emails, we do so because we want the user to think well of us. On the other hand, helping a friend who is having difficulty with a task is another kind of motivation. Again, motivation is when we read a business update because we want to learn more.

What is the best way for us to relax?

It's a question that's often asked but hardly answered. Some people believe that protection brings peace of mind. It's about seeking stillness and balance in life according to some while it is about acceptance and letting go, according to others. It all comes down to what we do, in our opinion. We just want to be happy with our lives. But there's no question that certain people are born happier than others. What is the reason for this? No one is aware. We now know that what we do and how we think will program our minds over the time of our lives. We will make ourselves happy by repeatedly concentrating on good emotions and events.

Eat well and some exercise.

Basically, whatever is good for our body is also good for our mind. We can also give ourselves a valuable mental message when we take care of ourselves by staying healthy and eating well: we are worth it!

Give your soul something to consume.

We also need to find ways to get away from the day-to-day work in order to get a better knowing of our lives and problems. Sometime we find it in religion, in music, countryside, or the seaside.

When we are motivated, our whole body is filled with state of excitement to help us achieve what we've set for ourselves, resulting in more energy. When we are interested about a project we are working on, for example, we hardly get tired. When we have control of our own activities, our energy levels increase because we are more interested about the result. When we are motivated, we are more likely to push at something, such as losing weight or finding a new career, and we will be pleased with the results. So, if we keep motivating ourselves, we will be happier than we were before. Happiness is the fundamental emotion that drives motivation, despite the fact that achievement is the source of motivation. Setting small challenges for ourselves is a good idea and we can learn to be content with small progress to ensure that our satisfaction and motivation levels continue to rise. According to one study, when one team member experiences and communicates positive feelings, others are more likely to react positively to that team member's attempts at social control. This applies to our personal lives as well.

Consider a moment when we spent time with someone who was cheerful; making us feel more productive

If that's the case, consider how our positive energy will affect those around us, making them feel more inspired. We would automatically be a better person and grow up if we understand what motivates us to do better. When anyone is inspired to do something, they are more dedicated to the mission and will give it their all. Let's pretend we are hoping for a raise. We have a great chance of growing and moving up in our careers if we are inspired and committed to doing our best. Motivation is essential for managing the difficulties that life throws at us. Highly driven individuals, for example, are well-organized, allocating specific times in their schedules to various tasks, and giving themselves deadlines to complete each task. Many who are less inspired, on the other hand, do not follow a clear plan. Something as easy as waking up on time and getting out of bed is a good example. We will be more inspired to get out of bed and into work on time if we enjoy what we do, but if we do not, we can end up hitting the button too many times, wasting time in the process.

Willpower

So, exactly what is willpower?

Willpower, known as determination or self-control, may refer to a variety of behavioural characteristics. What we want in the short term in order to achieve what we want in the long run.

Why is it important?

We had to find food to survive thousands of years ago. Living in a tribe often improved one's chances of survival, but it demanded self-control. We couldn't, for example, steal something that belonged to someone else without consequences. Back then, self-control was a must for survival, and it served us well evolutionary. We are all born with willpower today, but some people use it more efficiently than others.

Willpower, also known as 'self-discipline', is what encourages us to make long-term positive improvements in our lives. It is the inner resilience that pushes us forward through some setbacks along the way.

While there is some debate about willpower, an increasing body of research suggests that it should be regarded as a muscle.

In the sense of self-discipline, this means exercising our willpower on a daily basis but still enabling us to relax from time to time so that the 'willpower muscle' can fill its energy levels.

How can we strengthen our willpower?

Exercising can take us a long way

Thousands of people make the effort to exercise every day. They pay for gym memberships, commit for a few weeks, and then leave. Almost always, a lack of self-discipline is to blame. Commitment to sport calls willpower, but physical exercise is a best way to improve. If our willpower is low, we must trick our brain into believing that nothing is happening. If we are unable to take the stairs for all five floors, we must take them for one and then move to the elevator.

Controlling our food habits

We must choose between immediate satisfaction and a delayed but greater benefit later. According to research, a bad diet allows us to make more emotional decisions than a well diet. To that end, the same advice is to start with small. We may substitute tea with one glass of juice. We must keep making minor adjustments so that our brain does not notice a difference. We will easily boost our willpower.

We can distract ourselves

'Try to sit for this task ourselves: not to think of magic, and we will see that the blessed thing will come to mind every minute.'

We have to teach ourselves to think if the magic appears in our minds, we need to think about something else instead. When an unwanted thought begins to enter our mind, we may replace it with a good thought. This places us in charge of our thoughts.

Be realistic

There is nothing wrong with being optimistic, unless we constantly go all in. When we set something ambitious, we lose the game before we even begin. Set targets that are large enough to be inspiring yet small enough to be achievable. The sense of achieving will raise our self-esteem and our willpower.

Staying in a constant state of hunger for willpower won't help

Coaches and trainers in sports sometimes differentiate between comfort zones and stretch zones. If we are comfortable running a ten-minute run, slowing down to eight minutes, puts us in our stretch zone. Changing between the two is an effective way to enhance our results. However, living in our comfort zone forever is not a safe idea. Owing to a lack of recovery time, our risk of injury rises, and we suffer in the long run. The same is true for willpower.

Self-Control and Willpower

Willpower and self-discipline are essential in life for they lead to happiness if we have them or to failure if we do not. These two abilities are important for handling anything and achieving what we want. Good people have these two abilities, and we must have them as well.

What is self-discipline?

- It is our inner strength that allows us to work hard in our efforts.

- It is the ability to know physical, social, and mental difficulty.

- It means courage and dedication.

- It is the desire to slow down instant satisfaction, enjoyment, or comfort in order to achieve something better.

Developing willpower and self-discipline are two essential skills that will enable us to overcome laziness and impatience, as well as develop self-control and inner strength.

These two skills provide us with the inner strength we need for taking actions and continuing with our actions in the face of difficulties. They offer us courage to stick to our path. They also give us the strength to avoid doing something that will distract us. These abilities will assist us in changing our lives, losing weight, avoiding fast food, developing healthy habits, and avoiding poor habits. They are extremely beneficial to all of us. If we want to grow in life, there should be no excuses, hesitations, or laziness.

Let's go through a few questions

- Do we ever feel the lack of inner strength to act confidently or strong?

- Do we have anything that we would like to improve but due to lack of inner strength, couldn't do so?

- How many times have we wanted to make excuses to stay at home and watch TV instead due to laziness or a lack of inner strength?

- How many times have we wanted to change our food habits, or get up early in the morning but due to lack of inner strength couldn't do so?

- Do we start doing things and leave them in middle after a short time?

If we say yes to the majority of these, then there is lack of willpower and self-discipline.

Can we fix it? Absolutely.

How to break through?

We will improve this behaviour by improving our self-control and willpower. All we need is some instruction, direction, and advice. We will feel more strong, secure, and in control of our lives and ourselves.

- People who have self-control are more in command of their lives and actions.

- Self-disciplined people have inner power which allows them to deal with challenges and difficulties.

- Self-disciplined people have more willpower than others and do not let desires, emotions, and what other people say, influence their decisions.

Exercises to help us through the process

Doing things, we'd rather stop doing due to laziness, hesitation; lack of decision, shyness, or other causes is an easy strategy for improving. Carrying out such activities strengthens us.

- Consider that you are sitting in a bus or train when an old man or woman enters. We will stand and vacate our seats, even though we would like to remain seated. Act in this way not because it is respectful, but also because we are doing something we are shy to do. This is an exercise in overcoming our body, mind, and emotions' battle.

- There are dishes in the sink that need to be washed, so we put them off for later. Instead of putting it off, we have to get up and wash them now. We cannot allow laziness to rule us. When we understand that by doing so, we are ultimately improving ourselves, it becomes easier to act against our laziness.

- We come home from work and sit in front of the television because we are too lazy or exhausted to do some exercise or *puja* first. We must control ourselves to sit in front of the television.

- Do we like our coffee with sugar? If we do, we can drink it without sugar for one week. Do we have three cups of coffee or tea every day? If we do, we can restrict ourselves to two cups a day for a week.

- Do we like reading gossip in the newspaper or magazine? Then, for one week, avoid from doing so. This may not be simple, but it is beneficial for our development.

- If we have the choice of taking the elevator or the stairs, we should take the stairs. However, we can only climb the stairs if it is not on high floor and if we are in good health.

The exercises mentioned above are quick and easy to perform. The fact that they are basics, doing them strengthens our inner strength, which we can then use for other tasks and activities that need more inner strength. Exercises are there to establish inner confidence, not to make our life difficult. Weight lifting, aerobics, or any other form of sport strengthens our bodies, allowing us to use our physical strength anytime we need it. The same is with willpower and self-discipline. We make willpower and self-discipline available to us whenever we need them by preparing and improving. They help us in changing our habits, giving us more power over our lives, and providing us with the inner strength needed for personal and spiritual growth.

HAPPINESS IS...

...taking control of your own happiness.

We lack willpower, and if we feel the need to develop self-discipline, we should not hesitate. Start small; take small steps, and then advance. We gain trust and faith in ourselves as a result, and our sense of inner strength grows.

14. The Road to Inner Peace

Inner peace is possible, and it doesn't need us to meditate on the Himalayas or spend days in a yoga retreat. We do not live in a meditation retreat; we live in the real world after all. When we are waiting in line at the grocery store and the products of our bag fall on the floor just as our phone rings, we need to find inner peace within ourselves. The problem is that most of us work on the surface where there is a lot of conflict and confusion. But each individual has this deep and calm awareness. To find inner peace, we do not have to turn off all the lights. There's this belief that if we are in a quiet place, it will be easier to reach this part of us. Remind ourselves to take a deep breath, and hopefully, we are safe from harm. Consider the people we care about, as well as those who care about us. It's fine if it takes us some time to find out what our happy place is. We could imagine the mountains, our bedroom, a lake, playing with kids, being with someone we care about, or a favourite holiday. Our bodies will begin to feel as though we are still there when we access these memories, which will calm us.

Try taking a step back to see if what our brain is telling us is real in disappointment, anger, or panic thoughts. Examining the cause of our anxiety will make it smaller.

Now it's time to show ourselves some compassion and kindness. It relieves feeling of loneliness.

Gratitude comes before happiness. Happiness should not be a by-product of work or success. Performance should be based on happiness. Performance becomes a by-product if we are content and doing something we enjoy. When our satisfaction is dependent on our success, good things never occur. It's just a matter of concentration. What are we focusing on in our lives? What do we most desire? What are the reasons behind desiring those things? We know how much we are missing out or how limited we are to do the things we really want.

Living in a state of scarcity is injustice to us. We just see the bad aspects of life when we do not get what we want. We live in an abundant state when we concentrate on abundance and appreciation for what we have, even when we have to go through pain and loss. Happiness will never come until we are thankful for what we have. Even if we believe we have issues, we must be thankful for them. And, if we put our issues with people, we could be confident that we would win.

Others are still living in a much unsatisfactory state of life than we are. Lot of happenings are taking place right now in countries where people do not have the same resources as we have. We must always be grateful for what we have been given. Happiness will follow when we can live in a state of abundance and appreciation. Happiness and prosperity, on the other hand, will only be temporary if we can't be free from the state of scarcity. We will lose interest when we find something else that catches our eye.

Find something to be grateful for, even though we say we have nothing to be grateful for. We should be thankful for our ability to read and write, as well as our ability to think and reason. Family members, kids, food on the table, clothes, a roof over our head, and so on, are all the things for which we should be thankful. Nothing can destroy the present moment more than being in the past or continuously thinking about the future. However, many of us have difficulty being in present. We can't understand the present moment. We are typically more concerned with what will happen tomorrow or what happened yesterday than being in the present. What does it mean, though, to be present? What is the importance of this as one of the keys to happiness? Being present is like as simple act of gratitude. We take a moment to appreciate what can be seen in every direction, the beauty of everything around us, and the journey that we call life. It helps us in overcoming our worries for the future and past. When we are in present, we develop a natural love for life. This does not free us of responsibilities for our problems. Problems are a part of life, and there will still be concerns.

And while problems can cause us pain, big or small, they also help us to grow as individuals, learn, understand, become more understanding, and have new life discoveries. Being present identifies that we have issues but it does not cause our mental health. When we do not handle our time well, we are more likely to experience stress, anxiety, fear, and worry. We become so busy in the day-to-day acts of life that we fail to address the issues that will help us face future crisis and emergencies. If we do not control our time, we are more likely to delay, over-socialize, and watch television. Those time-wasters divert our attention away from our, long term objectives. As a result, when the things we really want in life aren't met, we become dissatisfied, and we also start to experience hopelessness as we take several steps backwards rather than going forward.

All of us have the same amount of time in this universe. We only have 24 hours in a day or 1,440 minutes or 86,400 seconds. Nobody has more time than the other, no matter how wealthy or poor they are, how tall or small they are, what religion they follow, or where they live. It is life's biggest truth. So, it's not how much time that causes us to be unhappy. It's what we do with the very little time we have. Make a habit of planning time. Do not let life get the best of you. Focus on our energies and develop a method that works for us, and implement it.

A powerful morning routine sets for the rest of the day. What we do first thing in the morning sets for the whole day. As a result, it determines the course of your life. If we want to be happy and prosperous in life, develop a set of morning routines to help us get there. The right set of behaviours and mindset can make all the difference. We are beings of habit and we fail to do the things that will improve our lives because we are too busy doing what we are used to doing. Being 'busy, being, and busy"

We are enslaved by habits and routines that aren't really beneficial to us. We are busy dealing with life's demands.

We need an empowering morning routine if we want to get ahead and feel mentally strong. Since our minds are so new and we have so much clarity in the morning, morning habits need to be implemented. We are also setting ourselves up for satisfaction by getting up early for healthy habits. Create a routine that will inspire rather than disrupt our life. Get up early, eat a healthy breakfast, exercise for 20 minutes, do yoga or meditate, set daily goals, and so on. Do not go through life in a rush. Take charge, take the control, be encouraged and empowered to do and accomplish something while still helping others and yourself.

Health and well-being are important part of happiness. When we hurt ourselves by over eating and so on, it has a negative impact not only on our bodies but also on our minds. Although it's fine to engage in those pleasures, people have a hard time leaving. The importance must be on health as a whole. The day should begin and end on a positive note. It does not suggest that life must be boring. However, if we want to grow in life, be satisfied, we must assure that we are getting the right food into our body. Peace starts with how we choose to live, our lifestyle, and what we consume. We must make sure that we do what our heart desires. This is the best way to find peace within ourselves. Anxiety, depression, and stress are issues that we all have in common these days, which is why more people are seeking inner peace. Inner peace, on the other hand, isn't something we can simply switch on; it's not something we decide to do. Inner peace is a state that can be attained and improved over time, a lifelong journey with a lifelong commitment. We all pay a high price for living in today's modern world. Smart technology, internet access everywhere, and a growing work culture that expects us to be online at all times.

Lunch breaks are becoming shorter, weekends are disappearing, and holidays are becoming something we save for when we retire. It isn't always a matter of choice. Because the world keeps running faster and faster, it never feels like we have room to breathe, to choose the option of slowing down. Trying to keep moving, on the other hand, is a self-destructive cycle. Mental health problems are more common than ever before, and suicide is no longer a hidden event in our social circles. Expectations and demands are rising, and we are no longer competing against our classmates, co-workers, or town; we are competing against the entire planet. And it is for this reason that inner peace has never been more important in our lives. We've forgotten to live a life of not being constantly overburdened, overworked, overbooked, and underestimated by others and ourselves. Perhaps in the pre-modern world, most people didn't feel the need to find inner peace as though it were a journey or a goal because the world didn't expect them to do so. The need for inner peace has now become a part of our lives because everything around us is disrupting our inner peace. Although many people find a sense of spirituality in practising inner peace and ancient teachings. While studying *Bhagavad Gita* and meditation can definitely help in the personal journey towards true inner peace; the concepts behind inner peace can also be very practical in everyday life. To understand what inner peace is, we must first understand what it is not. There isn't any inner peace.

- Allowing life to pass you by
- Never having any fun although remaining cool

- Ignoring chances to expand our perspective and try new stuff

- We do not have any more energy.

The practise of inner peace does not have to affect our outward appearance; if we change externally, it is simply a decision made when we have changed internally. But what exactly is inner peace? Inner peace is a spiritual and emotional condition. Inner peace is when the noise in our heads stops, allowing us to see the gap between our minds for the first time. In a world of continuous noise, inner peace provides the calm we need. It enables us to open our minds' eyes and see how everything has become. We notice why we experience the tension, stress, and anxiety that strongly affects our daily lives when we have inner peace, and we can clear out the messed rooms we've created in our heads. With so many people struggling with mental health problems, so many people go down in work, and so many people move away from religion and spirituality. The search for inner peace is a lifeline for millions. It's a way for us to take a step back from our busy self, who is stuck in a state of anxiety, and relax for a moment. Inner peace brings about achievement of satisfaction and contentment by reconnection with self, rather than by acquiring material objects. It also calls for becoming a better version of one's self.

Being whoever, we want to be, but a better version of ourselves, with the clarity and presence of a calm inner self.

Accepting everything about ourselves— our lives, our jobs, your bodies — so we can honestly improve for the better. On the other hand, being with one's own strengths and flaws. It's about being content with which we are right now while still being patient in shaping who we will be.

...realizing how good it is
to be alive.

To keep our inner peace, follow these simple guidelines:

- Keep an eye out for greed - Wanting more than we require would only distract us from your sense of fulfilment.

- Keep an eye out for defensive conduct- Be open to criticism from others without blaming ourselves.

- Be more open to what the future has in store.

- We must accept and enjoy what comes, in order to save our inner peace.

15. Happiness lies in the present

Time and our understanding of it is complicated.

We humans aren't very good at putting time in context. Our brain, unfortunately, is in on the joke: the way we perceive, record, preserve, and relive memories differs greatly.

Reminding and assuming have their uses, but in order to get the most out of life—or, at the very least, to avoid living for the past and the future at the cost of the present—we need to believe in the now as much as then.

We are not happy in the past, and we will not be happy in the future. We are only in the present, and it is only in that moment that we have the ability to, learn, grow, give, and impact.

The concept of right-now happiness is not dependent on future progress or past failures. It all depends on what we are doing right now to grow ourselves in the present, to feel like we are living the life we should be living, to relax completely, guilt-free, because we know we are on our way to greatness.

Each person should determine for himself or herself whether we are forced to compromise or whether there is a just a way to remain uncompromised. All living things, including the insects, look for happiness. Human beings have a more logical mind and more experience.

Given their desire for peace and happiness, humans establish triggers for suffering, misery, and unhappiness. And when we establish triggers for unhappiness, unhappiness will surely chase us. We hate unhappiness, so we still want to blame it on someone else.

In order to understand ourselves, we must begin with study. If we can understand ourselves, we can understand the rest of the world.

We live in a so-called modern, ultra-modern, or post-modern society—a civilization that prioritises external material things while totally ignoring the inner self, the inner universe. We are absolutely dependent on the Internet, and we have forgotten about the 'inner net'. We are all distinct entities as a result of the disconnection of our inner net. Our relation with other living beings, with nature, and with everything else has been ignored.

The planet is not in a good place right now as a result of our compromises of lies. Furthermore, human pain is being heated up by the Internet and the information revolution. Every day, we learn about what is going on in the other side of the planet. We collectively create problems, while in the past; most problems were generated by individuals or small groups. Now that almost every human being is generating challenges, we face plenty of difficulties. Any of these challenges has the potential to kill this entire small world.

Happiness means different things to different people

Let's understand this with the help of a story.

A monk stayed in a cave, didn't eat anything, and drank only water from a nearby lake. He spent his days in a cave meditating. Many years later, when he was at the lake gathering water to carry back to the cave, a tiger unexpectedly came up behind him and attacked him.

In an area, there was a businessman who established a restaurant chain. He became rich, and his restaurants became well-known in the neighbourhood. He would use his fortune to live a luxurious lifestyle, purchasing a mansion and owning luxury automobiles. He fell ill and died several years later.

Were the monk and the businessman content with their lives? Their perspectives on life were opposite. The monk was concerned with nurturing his inner self, being present in the moment, and attaining enlightenment. He was unconcerned with external goods, and only owned robes that he wore every day.

The businessman concentrated on amassing material wealth, amassing everything he desired: mansions, cars, and wardrobes stocked with high-end garments and accessories. He was oblivious to his inner being; such a word did not exist for him.

Could they both have been correct in their own way?

True, however the form of happiness differs.

Happiness comes from inside the monk, it is everlasting, and it is not based on anything. He is accessing the soul of his being, where harmony and happiness flourish through meditation and being present (known as mindfulness today). He was content on the inside.

The happiness of a businessman is from material possessions; it is entirely dependent on an emotional connection to them. His life is 'desire driven' as he uses his money to purchase whatever he wants, such as buying the house of his dreams or travelling the globe.

If the businessman lost all of his wealth and properties, his needs would no longer be satisfied, and he would therefore be unhappy. He was satisfied with his material circumstances.

Which is the preferable approach?

As the story goes, even though the monk attained everlasting peace, he was killed by a tiger. And the businessman had material success before becoming ill and dying.

Let us not take the story literally in the sense that if we behave like the monk, we will be eaten by a tiger, or if we act like the businessman, we will die.

What we need to do is find a happy medium. Living on the extremes is dangerous for the body, mind, and soul; seeking a balance where we develop our inner being while still maintaining a safe lifestyle is important in today's modern world.

Having happiness that comes from inside us means that if we do have additional materials, we will exist together with it. One does not take the place of the other because inner pleasure is eternal and cannot be replaced; it can only be hidden by wishes.

This is why we hear stories of the rich who have money and fame but are unhappy. They have not developed their inner happiness and trust only material happiness. They are 'the businessmen,' and the wishes they felt would bring them happiness were just temporary.

The businessman can have an effect on others through his endeavours, whatever they may be, while the monk has removed himself from the world for the sole purpose of fulfilling his one and only wish.

Why Should We Focus on the Present for Happiness?

We spend a lot of our time thinking about our happiness. Our thoughts revolve around the memories that lead to our happiness. The entire results are full of regrets. We always look back at our past and find something that we regret about. Then our thoughts take us to the future which is considered to be hopeless. We all have a habit of connecting the future with the past but we forget about the present.

"dancing"

The past is something that we have zero control over. We can make our future if we focus on our present. As we can see, the number one reason we should focus on the present to achieve happiness is to get control of our lives. The best way to understand this is with an example. Suppose a person had a very bad day. This bad day does not include a missed bus, but it makes the person think of their life decisions. Therefore, that bad day could consist of them failing an exam or losing a friend.

When performing improvement, one must be present in order to understand where things are going. When we are preoccupied with the past or the future, we cannot look for something really important in the present. Surfing, painting, writing, and even video games provide complete engagement.

Managing expectations

We can't enjoy experiences if we are always searching for individuals, places, and objects to fulfil our expectations and hopes. As a result, expectations can be a real happiness killer.

It is beneficial to have goals in life, but it is also important to keep them freely so that we can enjoy the fullness of lives.

How to live in the moment?

Life happens in the moment. Most of us do not approach our thoughts with awareness. Our emotions dominate us. To feel more in control of our minds and lives, to find the sense of balance, we must pause and rest in stillness—to stop doing and focus on just being.

Living in the moment, also known as mindfulness is a state of awareness and focus on the present. We become conscious as we recognise that we are not our feelings but an observer of our thoughts without judging them. Mindfulness requires accepting our feelings as they are, without moving away from it. People who are mindful are happier, more cheerful, and more stable. They have a higher sense of self-esteem and are more forgiving.

Being in the present moment decreases the emotions and feelings that causes depression and attention issues. Living in the moment with the hope of a reward brings about future-oriented mentality which disrupts every process. Instead, we must simply believe that the rewards will come. There are several approaches to mindfulness and letting go of our desires is the only way to obtain them. Here are a few tips to get you started.

We have to be present in the place

We must ignore the other choices and prefer to be where we are—rather than prioritising our smartphones over dinner conversations or late-night reading. Engaging in our present in easy and mindful ways has lots of benefits for our happiness.

We have to be present in the time

Achieving targets isn't as important as we think. One target and another, and by the time we achieve them, we've already experienced the joy of achieving. We must look less towards the future and more towards the present to improve and be the best version of ourselves, which will bring amazingly true happiness.

We have to step outside the daily routine

It's important to take a break from routine on occasions to slow down, to do something out of the ordinary, or simply look at the world with new eyes.

We have to stop postponing things

We must avoid putting things for later at the cost of present. We must allow ourselves to listen to our favourite music again and again. We've got to find out what makes us happy. Dance? What about paper aeroplanes? How about playing carom sitting on the floor? We must try them.

How can we utilize mindfulness?

It takes a lot of time to remain in present. We do not have to criticize ourselves for not being present. Simply accepting that we are not present helps us feel better and calm. Then it would be easy to return to the present moment. Going for perfection every time adds to anxiety and self-criticism.

Social skills are improved

When we are in present, our minds are no longer filled with past. With our attention directed toward the individual with whom we are communicating, we simply let things flow from us.

Creativity is improved

If we do some work, we might have discovered that our best work comes when we are not focusing too hard. We simply write, paint, and play. We reach a point where things just come to us.

It helps us release the tension from our body as well as our mind

When we are present, we have a sense of inner stillness. By concentrating on the inhales and exhales, we attach ourselves to the present moment rather than the past or future events that are stressing us out.

16. Self-Development is Key

'The only person you are destined to become is the person you decide to be.'

- Tony Robbins

Any change in our lives requires a firm decision. As a result, we must live a life of continuous improvement. Learn everything we can about our field, then find experts and contact them. Listen to all of the podcasts, and read everything we can about philosophy and ancient scriptures. We do not have to wait for something to begin this process. Something that is worth it requires commitment and action. So, get started on our growth today and put it into effect. We must think like a learner. All successful people never believe they have learned everything.

- Never be content with our present achievements. Never be satisfied with ourselves because we think we've achieved something. It's great to be content, but we can never stop learning and developing.

- Be a lifelong learner – This message is must for ourselves to learn something new. The good news is that thanks to today's abundance of free content, we all have access to information that previous generations would have paid a high price for.

- Concentrate on a few points - This suggests that we can decide which areas we want to develop and learn about.

- Develop a personal growth strategy - As previously mentioned, fix time per day for personal development. Only then will we enjoy the rewards.

- Pay the price - Just like everything else in life, development requires a sacrifice on our part. Of course, there are many forms of entertainment available, but if we want to grow in life, we must focus on learning rather than entertainment.

HAPPINESS IS...

...learning something new.

Though we gain information, learning is only useful when we can put it to use. So, act on and apply what

we've learned. Do we want to develop our skills in a particular area? It's worth reading about. Make efforts to be more meditative. Read books that go through this. Do we want to increase our productivity? We can start by reading which will always be on our minds. A mentor can be anybody, from a friend that knows something you do not, to someone who can take us to next level. Mentorship is the most efficient way to learn.

We must be aware of how we can change if we really want to take self-development seriously, and not just talk about it. And the best way to find out how to improve is to focus and ask ourselves where and how we can improve. The outcomes are dictated by our routines. We can't live one life and hope to live another one someday.

Self-development is achieved in some capacity with others. Spend time with people who are working in a similar area and we will find that we learn at a faster pace with them.

Self-development is difficult, so being able to look to others for guidance, encouragement, or even regular reminders about how to keep going forward on our path is valuable.

Self-improvement is a process that takes time. It happens gradually. It's not as if we just take a pill and call it a day. Self-improvement is a way of life and a regular development.

We all try to fool ourselves by making an illusion for ourselves. This is similar to saying that we want to be good at what we do but do not put in the effort to achieve it. Passion is something that motivates us to pursue our goals in life.

Many people go through life without having a firm understanding of them. There is a difference between wanting to be someone and taking the steps required to become that person. It's easy to tell people about ourselves, but can we push it up with actions?

It's never too late to learn about ourselves. Once we do, we will be prepared for whatever comes next. When we know about ourselves, a new path won't look threatening because we will already know whether to turn left or right. People place a high importance on education. To be able to do what we do, we go to school during our childhood, then get undergraduate degree, and then get medical or professional degrees, or go for further research. When we graduate and enter the workplace, many of us stop to learn, improve, and grow in our lives and interests. The most influential business people and medical practitioners, on the other hand, never stop learning, and we do not mean continuing education or board preparation. They are interested in self-education and development as a result of their self-analysis. They feel that they can only learn if they are able to put their personal and professional lives on different places.

Self-improvement and personal development are part of our professional and personal lives. Invest largely in self-improvement. A strong interest in life and relationships will also lead us to happiness. We have agreed that we can no longer wait for happiness or success; instead, we will go out and make it happen.

HAPPINESS IS

...knowledge.

A resilient mind

In both life and work, there will be difficult times. We need the skills to deal with difficult situations as they appear. Personal growth does not exclude all negative things from happening, but it does help us in dealing with them when they arise. Resilience allows us to never see the end of the universe. Resilience gives us the patience, knowledge, and courage to keep going forward. Something happens for reasons as a result of self-development. There is no limit that can stop us if we have this mentality. We would have more confidence and personal skills to deal with any difficulties. It is an unavoidable part of life to deal with change. We all face setbacks at some point in our lives. Not only the result but also the long-term psychological effects may be affected by how we address these issues.

Self-development will not always be about how we feel. Most times, it is about how we manage ourselves. Our understanding about ourselves will change once we engage in activities that lead to self-development. The only way towards an improved version of ourselves is to be constant. Being constant might not solve our problems, but it surely helps us to lead peaceful life and take own decisions. Happiness is a process, it always will be. So, instead of just focusing on feeling, we can try and do our best every day.

17. Mantras of Happiness

Introduction to Happiness

- It is a collection of the most important topics that are discussed throughout the book.

Where do we start?

- Life will always make us feel like we are not capable of things. It generates self-doubt and we have to get pass it at any cost.

- Develop hobbies to keep ourselves away from negative thoughts.

Difficulty in Our Way to Happiness

- There are so many obstacles that we face before we can understand what it means to be happy.

- The second section offers solutions endorsing the benefits of meditation.

Pain and Suffering

- Pain is cannot be avoided in our lives, but how we deal with it is important.

- We must not let the pain turn into suffering; we might not be able to prevent pain but we can surely avoid suffering.

Looking for Happiness in Peace

- Importance of time, the necessity of change, and the truth about ego.

- 'We can be going through a time of depression or loneliness but, if we keep our minds steady, it will be easier to focus on our object.'

Are we Happy with Ourselves?

- Mark a path to follow that will lead us to true happiness.

- Loneliness can absorb us, and yet, we can rise above it.

What disturbs our Peace?

- There are different agents that stand as a barrier to the achievement of inner peace and we must overcome the same.

Simple Ways that Lead to a Happy Life

- Introduced different suggestions that will take us a step closer to achieving happiness.

- It includes issues such as lack of proper communication, not engaging in different activities, and how we must review the context of life with regard to something larger than it.

Can We be Truly Happy all the Time?

- How happy a person can truly be.

- How to correctly associate ourselves with things and people in order to achieve our happiness.

Looking Within for Happiness

- Happiness resides inside us; thus, all we have to do is take a little preview.

- It also includes a list of harmful assumptions we make about ourselves, what it really means, and how we must avoid it.

How can we achieve happiness (through people)?

- An approach where we will be helping ourselves by helping others.

- Different steps to deal with our friends or family members, as a result of which, we will receive clarity.

Focus On What Matters

- We must not let our focus shift under any circumstances.

- We must let go of the negativity, and focus on things and people that make us feel good about ourselves.

Finding Happiness in Other Activities

- Focus on three topics: motivation, willpower, and self-control. These three aspects are known to be associated with each other.

- Motivation: how it can help us.

- Willpower: Discussed the ways by which we can strengthen it.

- Self-control: Discussed how to stay on track.

The Road to Inner Peace

- Inner peace is self love, self acceptance

- Walk carefully on the path to inner peace.

Happiness lies in the present

- Happiness means different things to different people.

- We focus on the present to accomplish happiness

- How can we live in the moment?

- Finally, tips on the utilization of mindfulness.

HAPPINESS IS...

...learning something new.

Self-Development is Key

- Understanding how our minds work and acting upon that.

- A resilient mind can overcome any problems that life throws at it, and how to make our minds unaffected to what harms us.

9 789354 726682